I0113356

OPEN SPACES

THE REFLECTIONS OF A NATURALIST

R. N. STEWART

Illustrations by Elizabeth Allen

PREFACE

THIS book is offered with some diffidence because it is a collection of memories. Fate, duty and inclination have taken me wide and far, have given me opportunities to see strange scenes and, for the most part, to enjoy them. To record these memories has also given me pleasure, and I hope that some fraction of this enjoyment may be conveyed to the reader.

All the experiences related are factual. In the chapter ' Blizzard ' some of the details are taken from more than one such experience and, to this extent, the story is composite. The setting, however, has not been exaggerated, as anyone who has been exposed to an arctic storm will confirm.

' The Trap Line and the Wolf ' has already appeared in *Chambers's Journal*, and I am grateful to the editor of that magazine for permission to include it.

For the rest, no claim is made that these chapters constitute a serious treatise on Natural History and, with this admission, they can be left to the judgment of the reader.

R. N. STEWART

CONTENTS

INTRODUCTION

THERE are many differences between the lives of city dwellers and those of the country. One of the most marked is the certainty of daily events which form part of the city dweller's existence, such as the catching of trains, whose detail is announced by time-tables, the accuracy of which is fairly well maintained. He knows when the shops will open and, until recently, the almost certain knowledge that he could obtain what he required in them.

The countryman has no such pre-knowledge. The farmer or the fisherman is quite uncertain of the morrow's weather, in spite of the meteorologists. The finding of a particular species of animal or bird is governed by no time-table in the sense that we understand those of the railway companies. It is true that certain facts are ruled by strict time limits, such as the incubation of a setting of eggs, but most of the rest are probabilities but not certainties. If they were of the latter class much of our pleasure would be lost.

If this element of surprise, and often disappointment, were absent, Natural History would be a dull subject. Uncertainty is essential ; success without it would be the fruit of dull labour.

The naturalist is in certain respects a research worker, even if some of the phenomena he observes are already over travelled ground. To the pure research worker a repetition of some of his past successes can bring pleasure as well as confirmation of a theory already held. The recurrence of natural events is so much more exciting than the recurrence of the passage of a No. 19 bus.

CHAPTER ONE

THE TRAP LINE AND THE WOLF

WHILST at Fort Yukon an Indian friend, one Isaiah, asked me if I would like to come round his trap line.

It was in early December and the land was fast locked in the grip of winter. The thermometer had registered 72° F. of frost for some days (colloquially spoken of as ' 40 below ').

A trap line covers a wide stretch of country and may be 20, 30 or even 40 miles in length. No particular species of fur-bearer is sought or tried for, any victim is acceptable.

These lines are very jealously guarded privileges and, though there are no riparian owners, a trap line once established is as carefully preserved as if the trapper was indeed the owner, not only of the traps, but of the land itself. No poaching would be tolerated and no theft of the catch excused. Nor would it ever occur to any of the normal inhabitants to break this unwritten law. The value of a good line represents no mean sum in dollars at the end of the trapping season.

The main species caught in this part of the world are fox (silver, cross-bred and red), marten (very valuable), mink, ermine, lynx, wolverine, bear and occasionally wolf. Other furs such as musquash (known as ' rats ') and beaver are not trapped but shot when in season.

Besides the main quarry, snowshoe rabbits are caught for bait. Unwanted moose flesh and dried fish are also used for this purpose.

There are several grades of trap used, as it is obvious that a trap to catch a mink would not hold a bear. For the most part they are gin traps, double springed for the larger species, single for the small ones. Snowshoe rabbits are snared and the moose are shot.

I had always supposed that a trap line entailed a degree of cruelty that left little to excuse it, but after having seen one in

1

operation some of my misconceptions were removed.   But there is a large element of cruelty about it for some species.

The snowshoe rabbits are snared by means of a springy sappling tied down, and any rabbit caught is jerked up four feet in the air and killed at once.   With such a device there is no cruelty.

The smaller animals such as mink and ermine die very quickly, thanks not to the trap but to the cold.   Dying of cold is not a painful death and does not take long.   Indeed the victim merely becomes sleepier and sleepier till coma intervenes.   Even the jaws of the trap cause little pain owing to the anaesthetising effect of the low temperature.   With lynx, bears and wolves, however, there is no doubt that great cruelty must be inflicted.

We started out from Fort Yukon with a sled and a team of dogs.   The sled was not heavily loaded, because Isaiah hoped to fill it with the pelts.

Our first objective was to go round the rabbit snares to collect bait.   This took some hours, first to reach the line, then to collect the harvest.   We gathered about four dozen and shot a few more.

Then we went on to the line itself.   In a line as long as thirty odd miles it struck me that Isaiah must have a remarkable memory to know where each trap was set.   Though they were widely spaced, they must have averaged eight to ten to the mile, but he did not seem to miss any, and he assured me that he knew exactly where each one was set.

The country was flat and sparsely timbered with jack pine and birch trees.   The foreground scene was made beautiful by the heavy hoar frost on the trees, the snow and the ice.   The distant view was dark and menacing, veiled by lack of daylight and unrelieved by the absence of contours.   The trail was easy, because the snow was nowhere deep and much of the route was over the surface ice of hundreds of small lakes.

We made good time and by 6 p.m. we reached a camp site. During the day we had collected four mink, two marten and a few ermine.   Next evening we camped at a hut at the outer end of the line.

On the third day we found a two-thirds-grown dog wolf in one of the traps. Isaiah was delighted. This, he said, was a great triumph. I asked him what he proposed to do about it and he told me that he would take it home alive and use it as a sire for half-bred dogs. Not only that, as wolves robbed the traps, there was now one thief fewer.

The husky dog is a wonderful animal but is apt to suffer from lack of new blood. The very best dogs are those in which there is a quarter strain of wolf, that is the second generation after a pure wolf parent. Here then was the opportunity.

It is better to have the wolf as the male parent, because a pure-bred bitch wolf very seldom becomes tame, whereas it does not matter if the dog is savage. It is condemned anyway to a short life of captivity and the husky bitches are put in to the artificial den when in season. A young wolf is desirable, because old ones very seldom accept captivity and, even if they survive it, they often do not mate ; sometimes they kill the bitches. But a half- or three-quarter-grown wolf can be tamed sufficiently to serve the purpose.

The wolf in the trap was in a bad way. How long he had been in it I do not know. One leg was severely lacerated and he was near the end of his strength. Even so the wild light in his yellow eyes spoke clearly of the danger of a careless approach.

The dogs had been halted some 200 yards away. It would have been courting disaster to allow them near enough to fight the wolf ; or to risk the temptation to join in while the wolf was being secured.

I must frankly confess that my own inclination was to shoot the wolf, I thought it the kindest thing to do, seeing its injury and knowing the sort of life it would be condemned to live if we were successful in taking it back alive. However, I had to help Isaiah since it meant so much to him and its sacrifice would benefit several generations of huskies and their owners.

We took two wolf robes, a spare parka [1] and some lengths of

---

[1] A parka is the outside garment worn by all travelling in Arctic Alaska ; it is made of a caribou skin, fur outside, tanned on the inside.

stout ' babiche ' (strips of tanned caribou skin) from the sled and went up to the trapped beast. The ensuing struggle was unpleasant, but, because of the exhaustion of the wolf, it took a shorter time than I had expected.

Its mouth was tied, as were the hind legs, and we put a dressing on the wounded leg. Then we wrapped it up in one of the wolf robes and put it on the sled.

There was no use in trying to feed it at this time. Not only would it have refused sustenance but we should have lost time. Actually our action was the best for the wolf because warmth was what was most required and the robe provided this. We finished the trap line and came home.

The wolf was placed in a dark cabin and its door securely fastened, not only in case of escape, but also to prevent stray huskies from entering. If they could have entered they would either have been killed or, in its weakened state, have killed the wolf.

The wolf's jaws and legs were released and some raw meat and a bowl of watered milk were put in with it.

Never shall I forget the look in the eyes of that young creature, a mixture of misery and defiance, yet full of a desperate courage, faced by what it considered implacable enemies, and ready to fight to the death. Once again I was sorely tempted to end the affair.

He was too weak that day to apply his remedial tongue to his wounded leg. Isaiah said that we should leave the dressing alone as meanwhile it gave protection and when he was stronger he would deal with it himself. For his weakness the cabin provided sufficient shelter and the natural resistance of the animal would do the rest.

Next day we went in to see him. Some of the meat had been eaten which was a good sign and meant that the will to live was still dominant in him. The milk was frozen so we took it out, thawed it and put it back. It was impossible to hand-feed him, or to redress the leg. Such nursing would only have meant that we would have been severely bitten or have to tie the wolf's mouth again, and Isaiah thought that he was now able to nurse himself.

In this Isaiah was right, because it did heal, though ever afterwards the wolf walked with a limp.

I did not stay long enough at Fort Yukon to hear of the success or failure of the breeding, but before I left the wolf was quite strong again.

All the times I saw him he never came out of the cabin, even though a small 'area of open run was built for him so that he might do so yet not escape. He never lost that attitude of bitter hatred for his captors, even when accepting their hospitality in the shape of food. I often wondered if other men saw in his eyes the message of loathing he felt, or the desperate longing for freedom that seemed so plainly expressed to me. Perhaps it is as well that they did not see it.

His incarceration was so much worse than that of any of our zoological specimens, which seem to accept their captivity in some measure of patient resignation.

Wolves caught and kept as was this one, do not live long. They may serve the purpose of their captors and they may father a few litters, but a year or less is the probable expectation of life for them. To this day I cannot but feel that it would have been better for him if we had left that trap-line visit until a day or two later.

CHAPTER TWO

The Tortoise

FATE once ordained that I was to pass an idle three months in the Beshik Valley in Macedonia. And it was here that I cultivated an intimate acquaintance with a tortoise and his family.

My abode was a rather larger hole in the ground than the tortoise required, but having no better dwelling the intimacy was thus more complete.

Before this experience my acquaintance with tortoises was not very profound. I had known one slightly as a child in a grand-parental garden. But beyond seeing it walk about sluggishly in a climate which it obviously disliked, and rapping it on the back with a small stick when it wished to sleep, we never became familiar.

But in the Beshik Valley there are a great many tortoises and the climate from April onwards is such that they find a joy in living, are active, repay a detailed study and, to some extent, respond to friendship.

It was not until April that I became aware of their existence, because until that benign month the tortoises remained in their hibernating quarters, buried some distance below the surface.

But one morning I was dozing in a sleeping-bag and felt an unexpected weight on my feet. On looking up I saw a tortoise investigating my abode. He was not very big, about nine inches long and five inches across.

He was obviously still sleepy and his movements were as yet sluggish, just as those of the grand-parental tortoise had been.

I lifted him up and his only response was to tuck his head back into his carapace and fold his hands over his face. Once tucked in, no inducement that I could offer brought any response from him. So I put him down and waited. After a time he took

6

a sleepy peep to see what was happening and to reassure himself that no danger threatened.

The tortoise when in health and in his own country has very few natural enemies, and his only apparent defence is to seek the protection of his armour and there to accept anything that may happen. Once I saw him deliberately walk over a scorpion, which, thus disturbed, made two attacks, but the tortoise did not seem to notice that he had been attacked or had caused offence. He certainly suffered no hurt.

Confidence between us was established very quickly, and he decided that my dug-out was a nice warm place and took up his abode among my boots.

Once April has come the weather in Macedonia becomes warm by day, and my guest would go out to sun himself soon after sunrise.

Land tortoises are diurnal and herbivorous. He enjoyed a good night's sleep as much as I did, though he preferred to rise earlier. Each day he became more active and was to be found eating young grass shoots near the dug-out during most of the hours of daylight. I collected some early lettuces for him and these were particularly welcome fodder. After a time he would eat them readily from my hand ; he would even come from some distance to me once he knew that I would feed him. His toothless jaws were remarkably efficient at grass cutting and the blades were cut as cleanly as could be done by scissors. Such was his confidence that after the third day he would allow me to pick him up without assuming his attitude of passive defence.

When held in the air his four legs, stumpy tail and his head at the end of a long scraggy neck hung down, or vainly paddled the air in an absurd attitude. He had an eye of penetrating brilliance, though I think not equipped for distant sight, but at short range it was perfect. After all, no great range of vision was of much use to him, as his head was only about one inch from the ground level, and the country in which he lived had a thick luxuriant growth during his wakeful months, so the distant scene was much curtailed.

He had been up and about for some ten days when he found

a wife. I was only made aware of this by hearing a strange high-pitched squeaking cry which took some moments to locate and identify. I am not sure if this cry was a method of speech or merely an expression of emotional ecstasy.

His wife was rather smaller than he was and I think younger. The courting lasted for several days, though I am not sure that he was always faithful. For a time the two of them took their meals together, though his wife never shared our dug-out. Then the lady disappeared, presumably to lay her eggs, and I was never sure that I saw her again.

In May my tortoise was attacked by ticks. These parasites settled under his tail in the only soft spot available to them. I do not know if he minded them, but, even if he did, he could do nothing to remove them, because his carapace prevented his head from reaching the back half of his body. I tried to help but with no great success. These ticks remained on the host during the rest of our acquaintanceship.

He accepted the hospitality of my poor roof all the time I was there, some seven weeks ; and, when I left, he remained in possession of my dug-out. I still have a happy recollection of sunny evenings playing with my Chelonian friend, seeking titbits of vegetation for his enjoyment, trying to rid him of his parasites until driven to take refuge from the rising miasma and its accompanying horde of mosquitoes.

CHAPTER THREE

TWO PLACES

THERE are times when places seem to exert on us an especial influence. For this to happen it is not necessary that the moment be charged with drama. These wandering influences may drift down upon us as lightly and as quietly as thistledown, and it is not until we are almost snowed under by them that we become aware of the phenomena. Moderate invasion of the mind by such influences of unknown origin does help to stimulate our power of observation, but overdoses are apt to have a drugging effect, which may cloy the senses at the time. The individual thus affected almost seems to be in a dream and incapable of free thought and, when released from this influence, is left with an indelible impression in his mind of the site and circumstances thus seen, no matter whether the hypnosis has been of a pleasant or an unattractive nature.

THE FIRST PLACE

The first of the two places is in the Western Highlands and is called the Mill Lochs. There are, in fact, four lochs all forming part of a single water system. The road to them is not easy to find even with a map, because the direct line of approach is not the correct path. A climb of some severity is required and, although there is an ancient track, it is now so overgrown as to be indistinguishable from other than the practised eye of the native. The first portion of the road to the lochs is steep, rocky, and in one place requiring both hands as well as feet to assist in surmounting the obstacles.

After a climb of about 500 feet the gradient becomes easier. At the half-way mark—the 600-foot level—the traveller arrives at a small hollow in which a burn appears. Its source unseen,

9

deep in the rocks of the hillside, it only comes to the surface at this point, bubbling out of the rock face and tumbling down a rugged course, to lose itself again in another underground channel a few yards lower down.

Just where it first appears in the open, there is a hollow of about an acre in extent, sheltered from all but southerly winds, and it is here that many red deer come to die, almost as if it was a spot set apart for this purpose, lonely, quiet and comfortable, facing the south-west and open to the setting sun, the kind of place that seems most suitable for aged or sick beasts requiring solitude at such a time. I have never seen the spot free from the bones of former visitors. There they rest,

> Left for the wind to make music
> Through ribs that are glittering white.

To be quite honest I do not think that deer have a set place to die in, but this one does provide shelter from the storm, water for the parched, and quiet. In consequence the sick and weary choose it to rest in, and some of them remain there.

As the ascent continues the trees are left behind and the surface vegetation changes to heather, then to grass with bare rock in between, all much broken by peat hags.

Both roe and red deer may be surprised in any of the small hollows that open up before the climber, only to leap or run away, the action adopted depending on which species is thus alarmed.

The deer here are unaccustomed to human visitations, because the way is solitary and is only used by an occasional angler or stalker. Even these wanderers visit the area but few times in a season.

At 1,200 feet the first of the four lochs is found, a narrow strip of water about 1,000 yards long and 100 yards in width, with an island in the broadest part. On this island is a dwarfed rowan tree, some old long unburnt heather and, in the spring, the invariable site chosen by a pair of mallard to nest upon. At one time in the past the water from this loch was used as a means of power, hence its name, and the remains of a wooden

dam at its exit are still there. At this height above sea-level
well-seasoned wood lasts for many years even when exposed to the
weather, because the fungi that cause decay at lower levels will
not thrive at this altitude. These posts have been there for over
seventy years and are still sound.

In the loch there are trout, rather diminutive in size, but
prolific. I have been at some pains to increase their size, and
only recently, with much labour, I carried up a new stock of
trout, fresh water shrimps and snails. It is as yet too early to
see the result of these labours, but the change of blood in all
three species should benefit the native populations.

The second loch lies beyond the north end of the first one ;
the two are connected by a narrow neck of water. It is a small
round-shaped hollow of about 130 acres, deep water on the south
side, weeds and gravel elsewhere, full of fish. Two burns flow
in from the north and east sides, both of them spawning grounds
for the trout. The shores provide some heather where an occasional brace of grouse breed, and once I found the ring ouzel
there, a comparatively rare bird in that locality. In spring sand-
pipers nest near by and a few minutes' observation will show you
where the nest is. They always choose the same bank to nest
on, and knowing this, I can generally find it without waiting for
the parent birds to show it to me.

Number two loch has bigger fish in it, quite why is difficult
to discover, because the food supply seems to be the same, and
access to and from each loch is easy for the fish. In times of
spate both lochs become one, as the difference in their levels is
no more than about two feet, a fall which is no obstacle to the
rainfall of the Western Highlands.

Here, too, there is a rowan tree, gnarled with age, twisted
by the wind and yet surviving at an elevation which it obviously
has never liked but was powerless to avoid, having been dropped
there as a seed by some passing bird. Such trees may be seeds from
fine outstanding parents, planted by blind chance in an inhospitable site, where the promise of the sturdy growth of their
forbears develops into a dwarfed and shrivelled specimen, a mere
parody of a tree, condemned to live a life of extreme austerity

in uncongenial surroundings, neglected and forlorn, until some
winter gale of unusual severity ends what was but a travesty of
the life that the parent tree had the right to expect for all its
seeds.

The bed of the eastern burn from loch two takes the walker
to loch three ; about 100 feet higher. This is an even smaller
body of water, and to suit its dimensions its trout are even
smaller than in loch one, but they make up in numbers what
they lack in size, and their voracity is phenomenal. It is, of course,
all a question of supply and demand. The food is insufficient for
the inhabitants, and, to make matters worse, the trout are so
small that no-one will fish for them. They are so small indeed
that, even in these hard times, no British cook will bother to
cook them. Any attempt to place them in a frying-pan reduces
the carcass to an inedible cinder. As a result not even the
angler helps to reduce the stock.

A further rise of 200 feet and the last loch is found. Number
four loch is very much larger, 300 acres of irregular shape,
contains three islands and bigger and better fish.

Number four is now the home of a pair of red-throated divers,
who have chosen one of the islands to nest upon. These birds
used to occupy another home, but a pair of black-throated divers
drove them out and forced them to adopt such hospitality as
number four Mill Loch had to offer. This aggressive piracy
occurred when I was a boy. One year the black-throated divers
appeared and seized by force the waters and nesting island of the
red-throated divers, who, thus displaced, came to number four
Mill Loch and have been there ever since. I encourage them,
because I wish them to take a toll of the small trout, as by this
means the overstocking is to some slight extent checked.

On the other two islands the kittiwake gulls nest. There is
no boat available, so on all the islands the nesting birds are safe
from human molestation. Foxes often have a den near by, but I
have never known them to invade any of the islands during the
breeding season ; I think they dislike long-distance swimming.
Sometimes travelling otters are seen on these islands, and though
the otter is not a habitual egg eater, I cannot imagine that he

would refuse them should his visit coincide with the nesting season.

Number four loch is well sheltered by hills on the north and east sides, a short climb up the steep hill face allows the climber to see all four lochs with their connecting burns laid out at his feet. Not only that, but the ground slopes down to the sea and Mull and Ardnamurchan in the south, the isles of Eigg, Rhum and Muck in the west; to the north the hills of Skye are plainly visible. A fair sight to gaze upon ; and on the very clearest of days the southernmost of the Outer Isles are faintly visible on the horizon.

So the eye may pass from the delightful detail of the foreground to a grander scene, on a greater scale, where what is lost in detail is made up for by the general magnificence.

It is very pleasant to sit on this hillside and contemplate the scene thus exposed, to wonder why the fish in each loch vary so much in their growth for no apparent reason, to see the bird life carrying out its daily task, oblivious of your presence, and, if the mood be upon you, to look back in time and thus try to imagine the same scene as it was in the beginning of the earth's history and its subsequent development.

I receive the impression of three time scales, apparently running concurrently. There is the short scale in which the fish, insects and vegetation live. Their seasons come and go, and for most of these lives the number of seasons is a short figure, the passing of any one of them leaves no mark on the landscape or on the other two time scales, except in so far that during their lives they help to compose the detail of the surroundings.

Then there is my own scale, longer in time and seeming to be moving at a slower rate. I am conscious too that my presence, though accepted, is really that of an interloper, one who comes to pay a brief visit, but can never be considered as an essential to the scene, even though I do own the land. To the Spirit of such a place human proprietorship is of no significance.

Finally there is the third time scale, that of the hills, rocks and water ; this moves at a still slower tempo, change affecting them is so long in coming, or perhaps it would be better to say in ' becoming apparent,' because the change is taking place all the time in the form of erosion. The rate of this change, even if very slow, is constant. These rocks have seen so many generations of life arrive, flourish and die, without in themselves being responsible or affected, that immortality might be attributed to them. Of course they are not. Erosion alone forbids immortality.

Their final end is not easy to imagine. It may well be that in the not infinitely remote future the ' heat death ' of the physicists is to be their fate, or, before that, it is faintly possible that catastrophe on the cosmic scale may shatter and disperse the scene for ever from the universe. Perhaps it is not well to dwell upon thoughts which, however vast in stature, are perforce melancholy.

Today the Mill Lochs and their surroundings are delightful, the home of a teeming shy life ; but all the inhabitants are there if you will take a little trouble to see them—deer, birds, fish and insects, and the vegetation ruled over by the two old and gnarled rowan trees ; and if these should tire you, the fish be unresponsive to your flies or to your skill in presenting them, you can sit and meditate, either on the detail of the busy scene before you, or lift your eyes to the vaster scene and merely rest and gaze.

The choice is there for the visitor, provided he has the eye and the mind behind the eye, to appreciate these things.

THE SECOND PLACE

The second place that I wish to tell of is in a very different setting from the first, far removed in space. The site of it is in the north half of Alaska between the Yukon and Porcupine Rivers.

Two of us were out on the trail making our way to Circle City—a town of 1,500 log cabins and only 50 inhabitants. We had been several days on the trail, when the weather which had been cold turned very cold. We were in a hurry, because we had none too much dog food left, for two days the ' sourdough thermometer '—a bottle of mercury—had been frozen solid. This represents a Fahrenheit reading of about 77° frost—personally

I think it was colder than this figure. If there is no urgency, it is usually wiser not to travel under these conditions, but, if properly clothed and well fed, there is no particular danger in doing so, provided there are no accidents.

It was in January, and our actual latitude must have been just about the Arctic Circle. We had not seen the sun for some days. This part of Alaska has a wide selection of wild life. There are moose, bears, wolves, wolverines, lynx, marten, mink, hares (known locally as rabbits), beaver, muskrats (the last two hibernating at this season), and a selection of non-migratory birds such as willow grouse, snowy owls and a few others, but it was outside the range of the barren-land caribou.

The country was flat and covered with jack pine, small birch and other scrub growth. The snow lay about twelve inches deep of fine dry powder consistency. On its surface could be seen the tracks of all these living things, each going about its daily business of finding food.

We had been travelling well ; the dogs were fit and the load was light ; we had two teams and two sleds. Our course took us gradually downhill towards the banks of the Yukon. About midday we decided to call a halt and on topping a small rise looked for a pleasant spot in which to rest.

Some half-mile away we saw one that appeared ideal and made for it. This place was a small hollow surrounded by birch trees, each one of which had its twigs and branches furred with heavy hoar-frost. Fortunately, when it is as cold as this, there is no wind, indeed if there had been wind we should not have been travelling.

As we approached this hollow it became apparent that it was considerably deeper and rather larger than appeared from a distance. It was of saucer-like formation and there was water at the bottom—at least there was an ice covering.

A curious feature I noticed was that there were no tracks of any wild life entering the depression. At first this conveyed no message to me. We arrived at the bottom, halted the teams, checked the dogs' feet and the harness and then looked around the spot.

I do not believe I shall ever see a place so beautiful as this was : the frozen birch trees, the little lake with its thick ice covering, the pink twilight giving colour to the birch trees, the snow, and the stillness—silence as nearly absolute as can be imagined.

> Have you stood at some mighty mouthed hollow
> That's plumb full, of hush to the brim.

But it is no use trying to describe it. It had to be seen and felt to be appreciated.

I stood and stared—then, gradually at first, I felt the cold ; in this hollow the temperature must have been some 20° F. lower than on the level ground. I then remembered that all the wild had shunned this place, it was too cold. To stay there any length of time was but to die. But oh ! what beauty the place possessed. Its influence was overpowering. In spite of the danger, which common sense and experience made plain, the desire to remain there was almost overwhelming.

That small Arctic dell was one of those places whose hypnosis was too compelling. The place was quite impersonally hostile to animal life. Well, we left it—rather hurriedly—but it has imprinted an image on the memory never to be erased.

CHAPTER FOUR

THE STALKER

RECENTLY I sat in the cottage kitchen of an old stalker's house, the room spotlessly clean, comfortably furnished, some books on a shelf, the walls decorated with several stags' horns on shields, from one of which hung his glass, that treasured possession without which no stalker can travel far.

The man himself, old now but still active, I had known since my boyhood. Looking at him I was reminded of the couplet,

> Husbandmen of the wild,
> Reaping a barren gain.

Yet the quotation was not apt, because the gain of his life was anything but barren. Though not rich in material things, he was rich in experience, knowledge and that kind of mental comfort only to be acquired by close and constant contact with nature. His life had so obviously been a happy one. Now that the evening of it was approaching there were no regrets in not having followed a more lucrative or worldly career. He is a happy man and is content with the life he has led, nor would he now, or at any time, have changed his calling for another.

Perhaps heredity may have something to do with this love of the stalker's life. So many of them have had generations of their forbears follow the same pattern of life. It is not difficult to imagine the small boy in a lonely cottage listening to a father, wise in his calling, learned in some of the secrets of nature, telling the story, partly to amuse himself and partly to initiate the child before him in the lore so dear to his heart.

Then the passage of years, until the youth is old enough to be employed as a gillie or pony boy, after which apprenticeship he must learn by experience and his own desire for knowledge. If the desire is not there he will not take to the ' Hill.'

Unlike some other forms of keepering, the stalker is often widely versed in the art of shooting or fishing. He has great opportunities, because in the countryside of his livelihood the sport is not so confined to the pursuit of one species as it sometimes is with other kinds of gamekeeper.

The stalker may start by becoming a gillie. The word ' gillie ' today is often interpreted as an attendant on a fisherman. This is not the original meaning of the word, which is a ' boy ' or ' one who assists his master in hunting.' A gillie may accompany his employer whilst fishing, but, if this is all his service, a more correct description would be ' fishing gillie.'

But to return to the stalker, the first essential lesson in his profession is to learn the use of the ' glass ' or telescope.

This is not merely a matter of extending the implement to its correct length, adjusting the focus and applying it to the eye. It requires a very much more detailed study than might be supposed.

There is the ability to hold it steady in all places and conditions, the knowledge of where to look and what to look for, the aptitude to transfer the knowledge the glass reveals to the unassisted eye, so that the country under observation may be recognised by unaided sight, and the registering in the mind what the instrument tells the observer. It requires long practice to become proficient.

Those unaccustomed to the use of the glass find it an awkward tool and gain little but fatigue from carrying it, but in the hands of an expert in its use many things that were hidden are revealed.

By the use of the glass the stalker acquires much of his wisdom. So often have I heard complaints from the uninitiated out stalking, that the stalker wastes most of his day gazing spellbound at what appears to be a barren hillside. But in reality he studies the line of approach, the vagaries of the wind, as well as the worthiness of the beast to be pursued and the difficulties presented by other less worthy animals, that may impede the approach.

The skill acquired is only attained by constant use, in and out of season, so that it is rare to see the stalker without the little brown leather case hanging over his shoulder. The function of

the glass is not confined to the stalking of deer : its owner uses it for finding foxes and wild cats, for observing eagles and all the other wild life with which he has to be and desires to be acquainted.

One old stalker of my acquaintance, alas ! now dead, was so wedded to his glass that I never remember seeing him without this instrument. He used it on all and every occasion; the hours that he spent looking through it almost made me imagine that he lived in a world magnified to twenty diameters.

I often wondered what his glass revealed to him. I feel sure that its revelation was more than what was normally available to less mystical eyes. Indeed I think he saw his God through its magic lenses and, although he has left the instrument behind, I hope that the images it conveyed to him are now fully realised.

One of the more peculiar pieces of knowledge acquired by stalkers is their ability to find and expatiate on good drinking water. No true stalker appears to lack this knowledge, and he is most particular in his choice of water, no matter if it is to be taken neat or to dilute the contents of a flask.

I used to think that this was a pose and a nonsensical one, but it is not. Whether he acquires a special sense of taste, or develops a profound but inarticulate geological knowledge I do not know, but there is no doubt that once a source of water has been pronounced as ' good water ' by an old stalker it has a merit far in excess of what this commonplace commodity normally possesses.

Where the stalker shows his greatest skill is in hind shooting, not so much in the stalking of the hind, but in the selection of the hind to be shot. This selection requires an expert eye and great knowledge. To the normal eye one hind is very much like another, but it is the yeld hinds that are shot. Even amongst these a choice has to be made, a choice that can only be made correctly after years of experience.

Most stalkers I know are well-read men. Perhaps they are not widely read, but the books they select are good literature. This is not a habit confined to stalkers, but having had many acquaintances among those who lead lonely lives, I have noticed

that one of the effects of loneliness is that it inculcates a value
for the worthy rather than the trash in printed matter. A book
to one condemned to live much on his own resources for entertainment, has to have the quality of being able to be read more
than once and still supply mental stimulus and entertainment.
No book lacking in merit can do this, hence the choice of the
more worthy volumes.

The nature of his calling compels the stalker to live a lonely
life, his house is often situated far from those of other men,
and he has to depend on his own toil for his comfort. He keeps
his own cow, tills his own plot of land and reaps the modest
harvest that the barrenness of his croft permits. One so placed
has perforce to take his pleasure in his surroundings and if he
cannot do so, then he is not by nature fitted for the calling.

In the literature on stalking he has been extolled by many
writers, but even this praise is insufficient expression of gratitude
for the services he renders and the enjoyment he can and does
so readily give those privileged to accompany him.

With the modern trend of civilisation it would seem that
deer forests will soon disappear and with them will pass the men
who serve them. In the not unforeseeable future the stalker will
have gone, and the world will have lost a humble but worthy
race of men, who have made an unforgettable mark on the
hearts of some of us, and whom we are the better for having
known. But more tragic still, with them will pass a mode of
life that was able to bring its adherents happiness in their calling
and great content in their retirement. There are not many
trades of which the same can be said.

CHAPTER FIVE

The Red Deer

The literature on the red deer can be divided into two main categories : one, the killing of the animal for sport ; two, natural history plus some sentiment.

Both classes have been well done, but they leave out some aspects of the red deer's life which might well be recorded.

The red deer has long been the quarry of the hunter. In a way this has been beneficial, because if he had not been regarded as worthy of chase it is probable that he would have become extinct in this country generations ago, probably at about the same time as the wolf disappeared from these islands. The deer might have been preserved in a semi-domesticated condition in a few parks, but apart from this decorative purpose he would have disappeared.

A small contributory reason for the red deer's survival is that there always have been a few people who appreciate his flesh as a table delicacy, but this fact alone would not have saved him if it had been the only value that attached to his preservation.

The stalking of the red deer is unquestionably a manly pastime, and its decriers for the most part have little knowledge of what in fact takes place and still less understanding of the principles involved.

Not only does this pastime bring out many good qualities in those taking part in the sport, but from the deer's point of view it is a more merciful way of disposing of the surplus stock than the best-conducted slaughter-houses have to offer. In support of this statement it is as well to draw attention to the fact that the stalked stag has no knowledge of the presence of his destroyer, a condition quite foreign to the slaughter-house. The actual shot in many cases provides an instantaneous death, and in those cases where a stag may be wounded it is rare for the beast to escape for any length of time, though it has to be admitted that there are a few cases of individual animals whose demise is unpleasant.

All these remarks apply to the case where the pastime is properly conducted. The shooting of red deer with shot guns and other unsuitable weapons can incur nothing but the condemnation of all right-thinking men.

That some people may not wish to kill a stag, or indeed any animal, is quite a well-understood attitude and one which must earn respect, but there is no need for such persons to partake of this pursuit, and of all the so-called ' blood sports ', this, when undertaken in a properly conducted deer forest, approaches as near to the minimum of suffering as we have yet attained by any other methods, either in sport or butchery.

These preliminary remarks are made in view of the fact that the deer forest is likely to disappear in the near future. The passing of it will be a tragedy, as once it disappears the deer will become extinct except for those few kept in domestic captivity for curiosity and ornament.

The red deer inhabits ground that is of very little use for any other purpose but his preservation. It is true that deer which are out of place can do some damage to other interests, such as arable land, young plantations and crofters' vegetable plots, but there is no great difficulty in excluding them from these places, and should one be more cunning than the others and discover a method of evading the barriers, he should be shot. But this is no excuse for wholesale and indiscriminate slaughter of other beasts outside the prohibited area.

' Are deer forests worth retaining ? ' is the great question that is pressing for an answer today. This question has become bound up with certain political aspects and, as this is not a political chapter, it is not proposed to enter into a discussion of the controversies from that angle.

If our deer forests vanish the largest of our wild mammals will become extinct in these islands. With their passing the men who serve them will disappear, thus eliminating an honourable occupation which made many men happy in their lives. To some

THE RED DEER 31

of us this represents a tragic loss with no adequate gain to anyone else which can be foreseen.

The birth of the red deer takes place in June, it is seldom that more than one is born at a time to the same hind, but there are cases where twins have occurred. Where this is so, the chances of survival of both offspring are remote. If the hind in calf has had to face a severe spring where the grass is late in coming and, worse still, a very wet March and April, she has less chance of successfully raising her family. My experience is that the most important period in the life of the deer is unquestionably these two months.

A cold wet March and April are the worst possible conditions not only for the coming generation but for deer of all ages. It is at these times that the older beasts are driven by lack of food to raid the arable lands, and it is then that the worst depredations are made on the stock by indiscriminate slaughter.

By June there is a certain growth of grass on all the hill ground, and provided that the hind has sufficient stored vitality she should be able to bring up her calf.

The first few weeks after birth the calf is particularly help-less, but the hind is a good mother and provided that no unfore-seen disaster occurs there is no reason why the young beast should not survive.

Very often the previous year's calf is still following the mother, and it is rather fascinating to see the two generations together. They manage to ' get along ' fairly well, a somewhat unusual arrangement, because most other animals, and many humans, find the succeeding generations rather trying to live with.

In the earliest days of motherhood the hind segregates herself to some extent from other deer. At other times the gregarious instinct is so strong that isolation is abhorrent to them.

The full-grown stags have no family cares and indeed seem to be bored with the process of raising a family. In June they eschew female society and live entirely with other male company. Stags are far more conservative than are the members of the most exclusive West End club.

The process of rearing is one for careful forethought during the summer months. Even when the calves are able to graze for themselves the hinds are careful to see that the best grazing is available and that no very great distances are travelled which would exhaust the young beast. As soon as the calf can walk any distance the gregarious instinct becomes more active and small parties gather together. Quite apart from the enjoyment of each other's society, this instinct is one of self-preservation, in that there is ' safety in numbers ' to give warning on the approach of danger. Several pairs of wary eyes and very sensitive noses are better than one.

It is a little difficult to decide which is the predominant sense, sight or smell. There is no doubt that the eyes of the deer are very keen, but they can be insufficient to convey a message of danger by themselves. A hind may often see something about which she is uncertain; she will gaze at it for some time. Provided the object is stationary she may not be unduly alarmed. If it is upwind she then applies her nose to the air and makes her decision on what this organ has to tell her. If the object is downwind, there are several different methods of reassurance she may employ. One is the steady stare, hoping to wear out the patience of the possible enemy. If this fails, she will pretend to eat as if no longer interested, and then suddenly bob up her head and indulge in another long stare. If by chance she is slightly alarmed and thinks that there is a possible menace about, she will bark. This action has two objects: one, it warns all the party that she has seen something that may be dangerous, that she does not altogether like the look of it; and two, the bark may make the object of her suspicion move and declare itself.

The bark of inquisitiveness is quite different from the bark of genuine alarm when the hind has identified real danger. The first of these noises is more questioning, the second is so clearly a siren of danger that they cannot be confused.

If the staring and the barking fail, the hind will move slowly out of sight, hoping that by the unconcerned retreat confidence will be inspired in the enemy, and then she will suddenly return to have another long look. This latter ruse is too often successful as many stalkers will remember.

The hind is a much more wary individual than the stag, and it is upon their acumen and alertness that the stag depends to give warning while he is with them. When the stags are alone it is the young stags that are assigned the duties of a sentry. Whether this is because they have just left the schooling of the hinds' company and are therefore more accustomed to the drill of protective duties, or whether it is a sort of duty expected from the young, is difficult to be sure, but the system works well. The young being the more curious by nature pay more attention to odd details in the surroundings, and are thus fitted to see and report on what may be passing.

Where forestry interests are paramount it is the stags that are the culprits and responsible for most of the damage. This is due to the fact that a stag grows a new set of horns each year; the process of ridding these horns of the velvet when the time comes is how the damage is done. A young conifer makes a very adequate brush and the stag requires several brushings a day. The process is quite ruinous to the young tree. It is only trees up to about ten years of age that are used, so that plantations over this age are usually safe.

Deer of all sorts will eat the tops of very young trees, but after five years' growth they are fairly safe from this danger, except in very severe winters.

The purpose of the horn seems to be veiled. It is an inadequate weapon for any purpose, but its significance may be its attractiveness to the hind, though this hardly seems an adequate explanation because a large stag of inferior horn growth is just as successful in female society as a stag better equipped, and the hummel is never without a female following. To grow a set of horns and then cast them, all in one year, seems to us without reason and a considerable strain on the vital energy of the stag. Nature has purpose in most of its actions, so I suppose there can be no exception in the case of the horns of deer, but what it is escapes me. The growth of horn reflects many details in the life of the stag, such as whether the feeding has been good, the adequacy and composition of the diet, injuries to the bodily system, and age (rather inadequately).

On the whole the horns must be a nuisance to their owner. This is especially so while they are growing, and should he be a stag that prefers to live in timber, however cunning he may be in carrying his head, he must at times receive some painful bumps. The growing horn is very sensitive until it begins to harden.

To see a stag negotiate closed country in a hurry is a lesson for any lady with an outsize in fashionable headware.

The cast horns are often eaten by other deer, presumably for the lime they contain.

Another form of their diet is peculiar. In very hard seasons in the months of February and March deer will eat ivy. Now ivy is an active poisonous re-agent. Small quantities may do little harm, but in large quantities it often proves fatal. It acts as a violent purge. The fact that it is a poison must be known to the deer, yet such is their extremity, they will eat it and at a time when their digestive system is less able to assimilate this food.

At one time I was an enthusiastic stalker, looking forward to each season with relish. Today I have no wish to kill a stag, though I enjoy the watching and the stalking of them. It is true that I sometimes kill a stag or hind if they enter my garden—a form of self-defence. The reason for my change of attitude is perhaps interesting, though the facts of any individual's tastes or change in them is not of moment to others.

It so happened that I was in Fort Yukon in Alaska one September. All the inhabitants of that part of Alaska depend upon the killing of game for their winter meat. There are no domesticated animals except dogs, so that in each year in September and October the hunters set forth to kill the winter's meat, which consists of caribou, moose and bears. This meat keeps for many months in the climate of that country. At Fort Yukon there is a hospital; they too have to have meat, so the doctor in charge asked me to kill it for him—an invitation I accepted with delight and enthusisasm.

It was arranged that I would take an Indian to assist and he was to kill his own meat at the same time.

We journeyed some 400 miles up the River Yukon to a very lonely part of the world and there built our camp.

Now having been brought up on a Scottish deer forest I had nice ideas about killing the best stag. So when we made a stalk and ' got into ' a small party of caribou, I shot the stag, whereupon the Indian opened rapid fire on the few hinds and calves in sight, killing three of them and wounding two others. I was very incensed and protested hotly. He replied :

' Look, we are here to get meat, the quicker it is done the better, the younger the meat the better; we've got to kill all we can.'

He was, of course, right. This was no sporting expedition for him. It was work undertaken in order to survive. I only realised at that moment that I had a simple duty to perform, and for the time I was a butcher. Well, we killed the winter's meat, built a raft and took it down the river for 400 miles. Since then I have never wanted to kill any deer. Even today when I surprise a hind at close quarters and she looks at me in startled amaze from a distance of a few yards, the look in those eyes, a mixture of fear, curiosity and pleading, I wonder, not at the change that has been wrought in me, but how I ever could have wished to destroy them.

Deer have to be kept down in numbers to reasonable limits. The economics of the land demand this. The most humane way to do this is to shoot the surplus rather than leave them to die. That other interests have to be protected admits of no argument, but in doing so discrimination should be the rule. If this discrimination is not shown then the fate of the red deer is sealed, and with their passing there will disappear another landmark of a pleasant epoch, and the country will be the poorer for having lost an asset which provided amusement for many, employment for a few and put to use ground that at present seems unsuitable for any other purpose.

CHAPTER SIX

THE SWAN

THE Icelandic sun was low on the horizon, the time nearly midday, fitful dark clouds drifted by and the lake was still shrouded by snow-covered ice except for one black patch of open water, the only concession to the slow awakening from an arctic winter.

No life was visible, only some dead frost-encrusted blades of grass, broken and bent in their pitiful endeavour to show the glory of a past season. A small island was visible without much snow on it: the winter winds had effectively swept away the soft white covering from its exposed surface. The whole scene was one of desolation, leaving the mind to ponder on the malignant ferocity of the arctic night.

Still, that one open patch of water did offer some promise that a more benign season was approaching.

The lake remained tenantless and would do so for some weeks to come, as if cloaking its hospitality until such time as it could absorb the faint heat radiated by that anaemic sun.

The day wore on, the sun dipped all too quickly to have made itself felt, and a faint shimmer of ethereal aurora heralded another period of darkness.

March was passing and the lengthening day began to be apparent.

Suddenly, as if sent by the brightening rays, two swans appeared low in the western sky. Flying with powerful, but silent, wing beats they circled the lake, examined the open water patch, now slightly bigger than when we first saw it, and came to rest on the open water. The day was windless and the ripples of their landing gently lapped the ice edges.

The two swans swam round for a short space, preened their back feathers, dipped their heads below the cold water and, the inspection finished, made off to the west again.

Two days later they were back on the lake and this time alighted on the receding ice which connected the small island with the lee shore. They inspected the island, inhospitable as it still seemed, but it appeared to satisfy them.

Late in April the two swans took up their residence on the lake, and it was then plain that the previous reconnaissance had proved satisfactory and, in their minds, the island was suitable for the nest.

The lake is situated far from any haunt of man and is seldom visited, chiefly because it has nothing to offer to anyone, so it is eminently suitable for shelter and sanctuary for swans or other bird life.

The nest on the island was started late in April; its building seemed haphazard, rather in keeping with the surroundings, but gradually taking form under the industry of the swans—a vast heap of dead vegetation, with no attempt at concealment.

Concealment would be difficult to achieve in the surroundings chosen for the nest and unnecessary, because the parent swans are capable of dealing adequately with any threat except those of man and climate. There was little to fear from man because he found nothing there to attract him, and instinct armed the swans against most of the climatic hazards.

The first egg was laid in May; the whole clutch, five in number, by the seventh of June. By this date the lake was clear of ice, but, as yet, the climate had not permitted any growth in the vegetation to become apparent. The mother swan spent most of these spring days brooding the eggs, only leaving them in search of under-water weed shoots for her food, and only in the neighbourhood of the nest. The male bird allowed himself a little more latitude of movement, but was never far away. Not that there was much danger for the clutch of eggs from marauders, except possibly from some Greater Blackbacked Gulls, but they too were occupied in nest building and other family affairs. The lake was rather too far inland to be subject to the threats of other birds. Any danger that did exist lay in the possibility of neglect by the parents, such as allowing the eggs to become too cold.

The incubation period of thirty-six days passed uneventfully, but the scenic change was almost miraculous. The lake from being a forgotten corner of bleakness in an apparently lost and forsaken world, now had a clothing of fresh herbage, modest perhaps and not at all exotic, but viewed from any distance looking fresh and green, promising comfort and food. The weather by now was more congenial : the days had lengthened until darkness was but a memory and replaced by almost continuous sunlight, not very warm by the standards of temperate countries, but a great difference from the frigid immobility of the arctic winter or the searing blast of the blizzard with its millions of ice-driven particles.

The family were born to a welcoming world by the standards of the country of their birth—five little cygnets dressed in fluffy greyish-brown down, almost as if they had been dipped in a large bag of brown soot mixed with wood ashes.

After hatching the cygnets were vulnerable to any chance birds of prey if they wandered too far from the parental eye, but a rigid family discipline was maintained just to circumvent such a possibility. No wandering raven, falcon or other bird of prey was given the opportunity of a sudden swoop on the young family, and none of these birds was prepared to face the might of wrath that full-grown swans can exhibit in the defence of their family.

It was an idyllic time—warm sunny weather, and very pleasing to see the young family happy together, playing in the water, sometimes riding on the back of one or other of the parents, all in harmony and completely content.

Cygnets are slow of growth by comparison with other birds. This is odd, because nearly all birds that nest on the ground are fast growers in infancy, but perhaps we notice this difference more with swans because they are so much bigger than most of the birds to which we are accustomed.

By July the growth of vegetation was abundant. All arctic countries have a rush of growth in early summer, to make up for the time lost earlier in the year, and the season may be all too short. The soil, much of it lava products, is fertile, producing plant life which contains great nourishment. The cygnets responded by exaggerated growth of their necks and legs, these being the parts of their bodies most exercised in infancy. The replacement of the nursery suit of down by feathers seemed long in coming, but once started the change of clothing was rapid, these first feathers still of grey and brown colour, as if nature thought it as well to provide protection in colouring until the cygnets had attained strength and wisdom to compete with a hostile world. Not until their full strength was acquired would they be allowed to assume the majestic creamy white clothing of the full-grown swan.

The education of the family was thorough within the pre-scribed curriculum, consisting of the search for food, the use of the limbs for such progression as lay in their juvenile power, and the need for ever-present vigilance against the threat of danger. Not that any particular danger did threaten, but as with all wild creatures a permanent state of high nervous tension has to be encouraged if the race is to survive.

Attempts at flight were not begun until the end of July, the first experiments being quite ludicrous in their apparent inefficiency, but, when analysed, all so obviously done with the purpose of first, stretching the unaccustomed muscles, secondly, strengthening them, and finally giving the cygnet con-fidence in his or her ability to use those wings for the purpose they were designed for.

Flight once acquired was at first confined to very short dis-tances, but by the middle of August quite appreciable progress was being made and distances of a mile or more were accom-plished with ease and without fatigue. All this flight training is necessary in view of the preparation for the late-autumn migra-tion, when a really formidable flight has to be undertaken.

There is a mitigating condition in the migration of acquatic birds which lessens the risk of the flight compared with land birds, as it is possible for them to alight upon the sea without fear of final and catastrophic disaster.

The family lived in the most complete harmony: little squabbles between two young members of the same sex were but games and part of the instinctive training in self-defence and expression of character, but had no lasting significance apart from their educative value.

By the middle of August the nursery days were over and the family left the lake. They could now be found on the grass lands near the river's mouth or on the saltings of the tide-way. Here too other families of swans were to be met and the life became less patriarchal and more communal in some respects, in that the future movements were by groups of families, though each family rigidly maintained its own identity.

After leaving the lake and joining with other families, the brothers and sisters of previous years rejoined the group, but only those as yet unmated. This meant that the family was now a community of ten or twelve birds—not perhaps a steady number because casualties occur from time to time.

So the summer passed in growing strength and experience of changing scenes and ever widening horizons.

The older birds began to contemplate the autumn migration. This is a serious business, because fitness of the community as a whole is an overriding factor and the journey must not be attempted until it is certain that the weakest and youngest are fit for it. On the other hand the start must not be too much delayed, or the food supply will so diminish or deteriorate that the whole colony will be unfit for the journey. Weather has also to be considered: adverse winds of gale force might hamper the flight by causing dispersal or fatigue and thus destroying individual members. A certain risk has to be accepted, but wisdom, training and instinct all came to the assistance of the older birds in deciding the programme.

September passed and once more the nights began to lengthen and the air to cool. Equinoctial gales but served to assist in the training in flight of the younger generation by providing experience in dealing with the various violent air currents.

The whole life of the community of swans is influenced by an instinctive sense of well-being of the group rather than the individual. The patriarchal system of life has been developed to a marked degree, the most obvious evidence of this being the

return of the younger generations to the family group after the
season's nesting period is over. Even mated birds and their
offspring will rejoin the parents and grandparents, though
whether it is the male side of the family which attracts this
devotion is not clear.

Swans mate for life, thereby showing a highly developed
sentimental instinct. They suffer the tragedy of the inevitable
loss of the partner at some date in their lives; their reaction to
this calamity is related later in the story.

After the equinox calmer but cooler weather prevailed, but
the feeding was now confined to the tidal areas, and in the middle
of October the migration began.

At first it consisted in further accumulations of families and
their movement to the south and south-west coasts of Iceland.
The south-east coast offers little hospitality to migrant birds.

These gatherings were not in themselves very large, perhaps
fifty birds in a group, but the total numbers were considerable.

The reason for the scattering of the individual groups was
once more the question of food. A swan is a large bird and may
weigh twenty pounds when fully grown. Being vegetarians they
eat a considerable bulk of food. Fifty birds require a large acreage
to produce all their nourishment.

It is difficult to discover the factors that decide the hour of
the take-off for the great flight from Iceland to Scotland. Favourable wind and visibility seem to be the most probable, but some
instinctive foreknowledge of conditions on the route or at the
destination may also be a factor in making the decision.

Each group of families has a leader or small cabinet of leaders
on whom rests the decision to depart. Obedience to the dictates
of this individual or group is absolute, the only exceptions being
in cases of sickness or injury. The hour chosen is variable. In
any case the question of light is of no consequence : some of the
journey will have to be made in darkness.

The departure is impressive : group after group take the air
mounting in wide circular flight movements. Formation at first
is not apparent, but as height is gained the familiar V pattern
develops.

At the start a considerable height is desirable, and it is possible to see the groups at what appears to be well over 7,000 feet, should the day be clear enough and the start made in daylight.

It is probable that the height is governed by wind direction at the chosen level. Also it is important that the flight should be made in an atmosphere clear of ice particles or falling snow; rain is not of much moment, unless the temperature is such that the condition that aviators call ' icing ' is likely to occur. So the leaders have several problems to consider, but they justify their selection to leadership, proof of which is available to us in the success of the migration and the survival of the race.

The preparation for the migration must be a most exacting time for the young birds, because they will be certain to know that some adventure is afoot. Whether a full appreciation of the hazards is conveyed to them we shall never know, but it does not take much imagination to think out the careful instructions and parental anxiety during training, followed by the stern warning that any falling out by the way will not be tolerated, and, should it occur, the delinquent will be abandoned to his fate; in the sea there are creatures that would relish cygnet as a meal, and no longer is there the immunity from attack that they have enjoyed until now.

In favourable conditions the flight can be accomplished in fifteen hours. It is difficult to formulate an estimate of its time in bad conditions, but I have seen the swans driven to fly at water level, which must mean very unpleasant flying conditions higher up. In the very worst circumstances it is possible that they may have to alight on the sea, and this has to be considered. Whether the decision is taken by the leader without reference to the other birds in the flight, or is suggested by another bird in the formation, we shall never know, but the initiative will presumably remain with the leader.

The flight for the young birds must be a severe test, no matter what previous training they have undergone, and on arrival they are exhausted.

But the end of the journey must be very welcome to them, as they find an abundance of food and more benign weather.

As the flights of swans approach our coasts they split up, each party or groups of parties dividing, to proceed to the various lochs in Scotland which the older birds have selected. Once this selection is made they return to the same places year after year and from generation to generation unless driven from the resort by some extraneous event.

One such site is at my own home. In the winter quarters the swans have to accept a closer association with man as part of the price they have to pay for our hospitality. They do not markedly resent this; indeed they trust man, but with reserve, showing no great loss of confidence in their security except that they seldom allow of an approach by man within gunshot. In this caution they are wise, because there are individuals who will shoot at them.

However severe our winters may be they seldom entail conditions which incommode the swans. Sometimes a few of the smaller lochs may freeze, but if this happens they leave for the period of the closure, going to one of the bigger sheets of open water or perhaps to the coast, returning to the lochs when a thaw occurs.

It has been my great good fortune to be able to see much of the swans whilst they are visiting us, and to follow them to Iceland over a number of years. I like to feel that I see the same birds in Iceland that have visited me in the winter, absurd as I know the feeling to be.

Our waters are directly benefited by the swans' visit, in that they keep weeds down to a reasonable level in the waters they select to live upon. They are not fish or fish ova eaters.

Although swans are excellent parents, after the young cygnets have made the first migration they are no longer subject to the same care and attention that they received when younger, though from time to time demonstrations of what appears to be affection may be seen. Should a mishap occur to one of the younger birds it appears to be accepted as unfortunate, but it is not allowed to disturb the communal life of the family. However an accident to one of the mated birds is quite another matter. Here is stark tragedy, indeed quite soul-destroying in its immensity, to the other partner.

The severity of our winters is never such that the swans desert our shores, but it is difficult to understand how they find the nourishment to support them. It is abundantly clear that the cygnets grow whilst with us, and the whole family must keep fit for the return migration which takes place soon after the middle of March. This fitness is essential and a considerable reserve of strength must be acquired, because when they leave this country for Iceland they are faced with some weeks of severe privation where much less food is available.

It is possible to provide some extra rations for a few of them which they will accept, such as old potatoes and their peelings, outside leaves of cabbages and other unwanted trifles from the garden. They never become tame, but acquire confidence in time and will allow an approach to within a few yards of the person who brings the food. It is clear that they recognise the individual, but will not accept his advances other than at the place where he or she has accustomed the swans to find the food. Any approach at other places is regarded with suspicion.

It seems possible that the swans know by instinct what the winter conditions have been like in Iceland. Sometimes they delay their departure from these shores till well on in April for no apparent reason that we can see, even when climatic conditions here are mild and have been so for some weeks. It is as if they knew that in Iceland the conditions were not suitable, and they wisely wait until satisfied that all is well there.

The return migration is probably easier in some ways, because the young birds are now very much stronger and the more able to undertake the flight which is no longer a novel experience.

By March the cygnets have outgrown the childish games that they still played on their arrival in this country, and at this date can be seen swimming and acting as if fully grown. Absurd as this sometimes seems, because they still possess their childish dress of sooty brown feathers and are only about two-thirds the size of their elders, the dignity of their carriage is very marked, as if they felt that they have entered the mature and majestic kingdom of the older birds.

The courtship of the swan is a long and complicated business. I only wish that I were better informed on the subject, but the difficulty of formulating any opinion on this intimate process is immense. It is but right that they should take time and care over the process of mating—taking a partner for life requires mature reflection before any decision is made.

The permanence of the contract seems to indicate that deeper emotions than that of automatic reproduction are engendered, and such evidence as is available to us bears out this supposition.

Courtship begins after the second migration, when the previous year's cygnets are no longer directly under the parental eye.

Parents on all the higher mental planes seem inclined to look askance at the young enterprising male, or the too adventurous daughter. But when the parents are occupied with a seasonal reproduction the opportunity comes to the adolescent offspring. But the attachments made at this time do not always represent the final choice. However, the visiting birds to a family group are eventually accepted, perhaps the more easily because the young family takes so much looking after that the last year's generation can now be left to themselves. But with one rigid proviso, and that is that no interference with the leadership is involved. There does not appear to be any wish on the part of the young birds to take active steps to assume the control, until time or accident makes it obligatory that a new leader should accept the duties involved.

Both the courtship and the acceptance of leadership seem to indicate a well-ordered and advanced state of mental ability. This is not a solution arrived at by modern generations; it has to be presumed that this state of affairs has lasted for a longer time than the human race has shown the same sense of responsibility and application. The swans have reached a stage in evolution where sentiment and ambition follow a well-ordered routine, but at the same time allowing the individual full scope for freedom in choice of the mate.

Serious quarrels never seem to occur; not that this can be stated with final conviction, but if they do I have never seen one. Youthful bickerings do sometimes happen, but they are affairs of the moment only.

Once they are mated the two individuals are almost inseparable and pass the remainder of their lives in apparent agreement about all things spiritual and temporal.

There is a small loch well known to me which until twenty years ago had not been the winter resort of swans, but one year a pair of young ones took up their quarters there. They remained the whole of that winter season on its waters so it apparently was found to be satisfactory. The next year they returned with a family of four cygnets. So it went on, several seasons passed and each of them saw an augmentation of the family group until they were twenty-three. I took particular interest in them and felt assured that the original pair were still the leaders of this colony.

I used to greet them in October on their arrival and bid them *au revoir* in March or April, hoping that I should see them in Iceland in the summer months when I went there myself. Nothing had disturbed the even course of their lives, until one day a misguided sportsman fired at the swans as they flew over him, with no apparent result as far as he could see. But one of the older drake birds was wounded.

At first it did not seem that the result of this shot would prove serious : the wounded bird could be seen swimming away from the others but followed closely by his partner, both seeking solitude.

Neither of them would take part in the evening flights to search for food or for change of scene. Time wore on and the wounded bird became feebler, but was never deserted by his partner. At the end of the second week in March he died.

The rest of the family group were by now preparing for their spring migration and in due course left Scotland, but the mate of the dead swan remained behind. She could be seen day after day resting by the dead body of her mate, swimming slowly round it, and when a flood finally washed it ashore she would stand by as if keeping a watch, waiting for a soul that was never to return.

She fed but sparingly and in ever-lessening amounts, though by now food was there in abundance. Spring came and with it warmer weather, growth of weed and other foods became plentiful, but they ceased to interest her.

The vigil lasted some six weeks. Perhaps in the end she realised it was useless, never quite understanding why. But the mental anguish she felt must have been fundamental, striking at the very roots of her being. It was clear for some time that with his passing no further zest for life was possible to her. She had allowed the family to depart. Never again for her that stimulating flight to the North, that ruthless strife against the arctic blizzard, that small ice-bound lake with its tiny island was but a sad memory and infinitely remote.

Then one day in May when all the rest of the world looked so promising, fresh and happy, she took wing. Out West she went, never looking to the North, higher and higher in a straight line towards the setting sun. Soon all land had disappeared for her, but still she flew on as if searching in that vast red sunset for him whom she had lost. Even her great wings at last began to falter, due to fasting and perhaps sorrow; slowly she lost height. It seemed a long time before she reached the sea, a very lonely sea, making a V-shaped wake as she landed.

The sea was calm as if waiting to receive her and in sympathy with her mood. That stately grace she used to possess was now gone, the lovely curves of that neck were not now bent in pride but in despair. Slowly her head came to rest on the water, and by the time the last rays of the sun had disappeared her spirit passed with them.

Her death was in its way magnificent by its solitary grandeur, and could only have been encompassed by a broken heart.

CHAPTER SEVEN

THE GOLDEN PLOVER

THE golden plover lays eggs that are delightful to look at both in shape and colour. They are probably excellent eating, but I have never tried them. I still have the schoolboy's fascination for birds' eggs, though I no longer collect them. They are such a delicate work of art, only to be used for so short a time and then ruthlessly discarded like a piece of jetsam of no value, having served their brief purpose. No bird can afford, or even seems to feel a sentiment for baby clothes, and no egg shell can serve more than one chick.

Whilst wandering along the banks of an Icelandic river late in July, I disturbed a golden plover. As she had sat very tight I went to see what occupied her and found she had a nest with four eggs. Whether this was a second brood, which seems unlikely, or some tragedy had befallen her first nest, cannot be known. Perhaps she was one of the late starters in life.

Whatever the reason she was very busy doing her best to raise a family. The site was typical, on a tuft of moss in the tundra, raised some few inches above the mean level and well hidden in spite of the lack of cover; indeed had I not put her up, she would have escaped observation altogether. In order to keep an eye on the nest I had to mark the spot with a small cairn of stones.

By this date all the other golden plover had reared their families, and their chief concern at this time was in seeing that the young birds were taught how to behave, find their food and in the early training for the autumn migration.

The middle of July is, as a rule, a benign season, so perhaps this bird thought that it was pleasanter to sit in warm sunshine rather than the cold northerly winds off the ice-pack which prevailed in June. But in arctic countries the summer season is

short. Birds hatched in early August will be expected to be ready for the migratory flight in October. It seemed as if this brood were likely to start life severely handicapped.

Security in infancy seemed assured, but sweet as may be the summer, autumn brings cold winds, night frosts, wet snow (a very chilling substance) and ever diminishing daylight, all symptoms heralding the approach and severity of the arctic winter.

However arduous the mother may be in her maternal attentions, the eggs in their hatching will not be hurried, nor does it seem possible that the process of building strength, storing fat and youthful schooling can be hurried. There is one saving clause in the golden plover's migration. Unlike other species, all the birds do not start at one time; the departure is in groups spread over some weeks. So by taking her family to one of the last groups she might just be in time, but she will have a very anxious summer and early autumn, harassed by the thought that the chicks will not be ready.

There seems such purpose in the parental care of the golden plover, the male bird taking his full share in brooding and in the after care of the young birds, that I think they must have developed a sense of foresight for the future.

The hatching of these eggs occurred on 8 August. The young birds were healthy and strong. I saw them for a few days afterwards, then they disappeared, but I was greatly impressed by the progress they made, and before their final departure I felt somewhat reassured as to their future.

The golden plover's nest, although of very simple construction and employing practically no material other than what is on the site at the time of construction, is yet one of the neatest that I know of and looks supremely snug and comfortable. But as soon as the clutch is hatched and the young birds leave the nest, it deteriorates almost at once, and were it not for the broken egg shells it would be impossible to say that a nest had been there and that the brooding was successful. This rapid deterioration occurs with nearly all ground-built nests, but other than those in sand or stones, where any permanency is impossible,

I know of no nests which revert to normal ground so quickly as does that of the golden plover.

I shall never know the end of this bird's story, but at least I can wish the family well, even if imprudence was the cause of the delayed start.

CHAPTER EIGHT

The Black-Throated Diver

THE black-throated diver though widely distributed in north-western Scotland is not numerous. The habitation and breeding grounds of their choice are as a rule isolated, so, though available for study, they have escaped the attention that undoubtedly would have been theirs had they possessed more sociable habits or were more prolific.

In appearance the black-throated diver is striking rather than beautiful. His head, neck and throat are patterned with a contrast of shades that might almost be artificial, except that the detail of the shades is so exact that it is difficult to imagine an artist capable of producing the effect obtained. Perhaps the patience of an oriental painter of great skill might portray their delicacy. One curious feature about their neck feathers is that immersion in water enhances the contrast, whereas in most other birds saturation by water has the opposite effect and tends to produce a blending of all the colours and shades into an indeterminate and subdued whole.

I have a loch on which for many years the black-throated divers have nested. They came unannounced, and by aggression dispossessed the red-throated divers who had, for an unknown number of years before, looked upon this loch as their undisputed territory. Not only did the black-throated divers drive the red-throated divers away, but seized the nesting island and the very nest itself for their own use.

This island is of a curious formation. It is in fact only a tangled mass of floating weed, insufficient in density to bear the weight of a man, but firm enough for the birds. Weed and rushes flourish upon it, and each season's growth forms a stouter base for those to follow, like the formation of a coal or peat seam, adding a layer of rotted vegetable matter year by year.

When I was a boy this island was in another part of the loch, but in forty years it has moved about a mile. I think it has now come to a permanent resting-place and is finally anchored to the ground, as it has not moved for several years.

The black-throated divers are lonely birds. They are only seen in pairs, except for the brief weeks of the rearing season, when the young birds are with their parents.

I suspect that they mate for life and find sufficient intercourse with their own kind in marital bliss in an otherwise solitary world. They are good parents, until the young are capable of independence, when from being kindly guardians and capable teachers they suddenly change their natures, becoming bored with the young birds and driving them from the family home.

The young thus turned out into the world at large, have to seek another home. I have a feeling that this process of launching the young family into the world has as motive force the fear that the young birds will steal the loch and the nesting site. In other words it is a housing-shortage problem.

If my supposition is correct and the black-throated divers do mate for life, where is the mate found ? Because it seems too improbable that sister marries brother for generation after generation. Such inbreeding would have destroyed the race much earlier in its history. They must at some time and place have the opportunity to meet other members of their species, so perhaps the isolation sought by the mated couple is a post-marital trait.

The nest of the black-throated diver is no great structure, nor do the birds show any architectural skill or ideas in its design. It is just a trodden mass of sodden vegetation, damp at all times and often quite water-logged. There is no attempt at conceal-ment, which leads me to suppose that the parent birds are not subject to the fear of molestation by egg looters. They display caution on the approach of man, quietly sliding down a well-worn pathway from the nest into the water, and there diving with a lissomness that leaves scarcely a ripple behind them, to bob up perhaps twenty or thirty yards away and there to watch the intruder. During the nesting season they dislike taking wing when alarmed, much preferring to seek security by means of the

dive, and it has to be admitted that for most of the threats that they might be subject to, the dive does provide security.

With the birds on the loch that I know best, the site of the nest is very secure from any molestation, because no approach is possible from the shore. The mud which isolates the island is so soft that not even a fox would attempt the passage. Man can approach by boat, but the divers can hardly be expected to consider this possibility, or to guard against it ; also the boat is seldom seen as there is only one on the loch. There are no other threats except the possible discovery of the unguarded eggs by a hoodie crow or a black-backed gull whilst the parents are absent, but the brooding bird is seldom more than a few yards away and they are more than able to deal with any wandering hoodie crow bent upon egg stealing.

I have often taken the boat up to the nest and never have I found this action to do any harm. The old birds seem to show no great alarm and I have never known them to desert the nest.

However, once the young are hatched and in the water, no close approach is tolerated, the stronger they become the farther is the distance they like to keep from any stranger.

During the breeding season, and for some time after, the diet must consist largely of trout, though frogs, newts and other water insects will provide some change in the menu. I have seen the parents feed small trout to the young, but the days when such observation is possible are few, partly because the young birds leave the nest soon after hatching and the distance to this loch is considerable.

The divers of all species are great fishermen. The sensation of a young trout when confronted with that spearlike beak, the unblinking stare of that remorseless eye, and a body of solid streamlined muscle armed with propelling limbs of remarkable proficiency, might well form the subject of a trout nightmare and, what is worse, a dream that may often become reality.

During the winter months the divers are forced to seek their food farther afield. The lochs though not permanently frozen may be, and often are, frozen for some days or even weeks, which leaves only the sea available as a source of food for many of the divers. Others can and do visit the largest variety of lochs which seldom freeze in their entirety and where food is to be found. But I cannot imagine that any small loch can provide food in sufficient quantities during the winter months.

Few species of birds live the life of loneliness that the divers do. The eagle and many other of the falcons undergo long periods of isolation, but there are times when two or more of them are gathered together, and for a short season they take pleasure in the company of their kind. But it has never been my experience to see the divers of any species do likewise. This seems to imply that self-sufficiency is developed to a remarkable degree.

I should like to know the answers to the following queries. What happens when one of the pair dies ? Does the surviving partner die of a broken heart ? Or does he or she, prove less faithful than the swan, and depart in search of another mate ? Only a system of marking the birds would supply the answer.

The cry of the black-throated diver is harsh and penetrating, and can be heard over great distances. This cry from afar may be either a warning or a greeting, but discloses the presence of the bird to friend or foe. This suggests that foes must be few, because creatures that are exposed to many natural enemies generally possess voices less liable to attract attention than the raucous KAK—KAK—KAK of the black-throated diver.

The flight is of the rapid-wing-beat variety, giving the impression that they are in a desperate hurry, but this action is forced on them by the short wing having to deal with a body heavy for its size. All the birds that have the diving habit fully developed are forced to acquire this flight action.

On land they are clumsy : their legs, ill-designed for walking, only propel them at a clumsy wobble, but as they seldom allow themselves to be far from water they have little need to run, and if surprised whilst on shore, the few moments of ludicrous wobble is replaced by a symmetry of movement, when water-borne, that can only arouse admiration in the mind of the spectator.

It is expecting too much to ask that they should be efficient and graceful in progress in three mediums. In fact I know of no bird or animal that has the characteristic of graceful and efficient movement by air, by land and by water.

CHAPTER NINE

The Merganser

I AM in two minds about the attitude to adopt in writing about the merganser. As an angler he is one of my worst enemies, and I do what I can to encompass his destruction in and out of season. As a naturalist I find the bird has many engaging qualities, is interesting and, though on close inspection is of evil countenance, I cannot help feeling a sneaking admiration for him.

I will try to be fair, even if we are still to remain sworn enemies.

In appearance I have said that he is unsightly, but this is perhaps too sweeping. His face is evil, in that he has a sharp pointed. red beak, sawlike in construction, piercing red eyes with a fixed stare and a brick-red crest, this combination giving him that ferocious look. This expression is only apparent when he is looked at head on or full in the face, and is only noticeable when the bird is seen at close range. But apart from this, the drake merganser is very beautifully clothed and in winter plumage he is undoubtedly handsome, both at rest and in flight.

His flight is of the rapid-wing-beat variety, as if he was always just a little late in starting, or pursued by some enemy from whom he is desperately in need to escape. This flight is never varied, giving an impression of perpetual haste.

But let us begin at the beginning. The merganser nests in a hole in the ground : a disused rabbit hole is suitable, failing this a hollow under a large rock or stone will do.

I once saw a rabbit take refuge in a hole in which a merganser was nesting. The incident occurred when my dog put up the rabbit, which, in unreasoned flight, took refuge in the old hole to the alarm, disgust and fury of the brooding bird.

The site chosen by the merganser is as a rule close to salt water. They contrive to make at least one and sometimes two covered runways from the entrance of the nest to the water's edge, or as near to it as possible, by which they can sneak down and slide unobserved into the water. There is no doubt that this enables them to escape undue attention. The runway is admirably contrived, every use being made of natural conditions, and sometimes a tortuous course is chosen.

The nest may well be some height above the highest tides. Whether this is for security or for some other reason I do not know. The eggs—ten to thirteen in number, light greenish-blue in colour—are well protected with down. The nest is usually some feet in from the entrance.

Mergansers are excellent parents and have a care for their families which is remarkable, a fact which lessens my distaste for the bird. The duck merganser will look after the young brood for some time after the birds can fly. If expression or looks are any guide, I cannot help feeling that the merganser though efficient must be a severe parent—that ferocious stare and erected crest bodes ill for any disobedient member of the family, but facial features may be deceiving to non-mergansian eyes.

I have often watched a family on some of the pools of my river in Iceland when I have been fishing, and have had to admire the precaution the parent takes to preserve the young family against any attempt by me to interfere, not that at this time I have any weapon or intention to interfere in any way. No great alarm is displayed on my appearance or even my approach to within thirty yards, but any closer approach is treated with suspicion and the family are carefully shepherded out of harm's way. The young mergansers born on the shores of the sea or salt-water loch soon find their way to the river, where they learn various evil ways of catching the young of salmon and trout.

The initial feeding is one of regurgitation by the parents, and like all salt-water-bred birds they have an insatiable appetite. This is odd, because most inland-feeding birds do not wish to eat all their wakeful hours. The parent birds are persistent fresh-water-fish eaters, and even in infancy the young family is given a diet of salmon and trout fry, the parents taking lengthy trips to fresh water to gather this harvest.

The diving ability is remarkable : I have timed submergences

of over four minutes, which, when the lung capacity is considered, is an astounding length of time. Longer periods of submersion are possible when the birds are in danger, but this perhaps is not so remarkable.

In nearly every case the hunting dive is made in a straight line ; the bird will reappear in line with the entry of the beak. The dive is interesting to watch, because no special caution is taken before the dive, but the moment it is over and the bird appears on the surface, the closest scrutiny is made to see if all is safe and that no enemy has suddenly appeared. Once this scrutiny is over, he will swim about quite unconcernedly until the next dive.

If the depth and area of the water permits, the birds will dive as a means of escape in preference to flight. Why they do this is not easy to understand, because the fastest dive and swim is much slower than the slowest flight, and the distance placed between themselves and the enemy is also much less in diving than it is by flight. They use their wings under water as a means of propulsion, and the underwater progress is rapid and very efficient.

They are capable of taking a sea-trout finnoc [1] and swallowing it, nor will one satisfy their appetite. Like the cormorant I fully believe that the merganser is able to swallow more than his own weight of fish and still be capable of becoming air-borne.

The drake merganser has some very useful feathers for the tying of flies, the speckled feathers of the back, sides and rump make excellent substitute for teal wings.

Much as I detest the bird on my river I cannot help feeling a sneaking liking for him, but how I wish he would develop a taste for some other fish than salmon or trout. The merganser knows only too well just when the salmon ova hatch and the fry season is at its height, also when the shoals of smolts collect for their first sea migration. It is at this time that a special watch should be kept on the river to try and thwart their rapacity. It may be said in the merganser's favour that he is also fully aware of the elver run about the end of April, and he takes a heavy toll of these fish, which I, for one, do not begrudge him.

[1] The grilse stage of the sea-trout, on its return to fresh water after one summer at sea ; other common names are herling or whitling.

CHAPTER TEN

TREES

IN the primeval forest nature in its raw state is very evident. There is at first glance abysmal confusion : fine upstanding trees in the prime of their lives, old and dying trees, dead trees in various stages of decay and young trees struggling through a mass of corpses and other stultifying vegetation, held together by such a network of creepers that it seems miraculous that they survive. The whole scene is one of apparent chaos and disorder of intertwined lianas, dead branches, rotting trunks and general debris, yet with some purpose and design behind the medley.

All natural processes are extravagant in their preparation, but there can be no failure to discover that even in this extravagance the final result represents a form of efficiency.

If an observer of such a scene allowed himself to dwell upon it, it is in some ways a melancholy one. The human mind has been brought up to abhor waste and profligacy, but nature is bound by other, no less rigid, rules which appal the trained economist.

The natural forests of today are but a relic of what the world was like in an earlier epoch, before the hand of man came and spread a not too attractive veneer called civilisation over the spaces.

Man is the only living creature who can be devastatingly destructive to all forms of life. It is, of course, true that previous to man there existed both animals and plants which have disappeared for ever from this world and whose disappearance is not due to the action of man. Climatic change has been the principal cause of their disappearance. These cases represent a stage in the course of evolution through which our planet has inevitably to pass, and will continue as long as the planet remains a home for living creatures.

The trees that most of us know are not faced with the conditions that prevail in virgin forests. They are cultivated plants, some have more care and attention paid them than others, and the results we see vary from complete neglect to mutilation in order to fit them into some corner too small for their stature.

The primary object of recent afforestation has been for the production of a raw material, and however pleasant it may be to see and handle well-made articles of fine wood, this pleasure is only to be enjoyed by the death of the plant that provides it. To the naturalist it is the growing tree that provides his pleasure, not the corpses, or their market value.

I was walking down the tree-lined boulevard of a Continental city when I came on a party of city foresters pollarding the plane trees. I stopped to watch, because the surgeon of the party was at the moment occupied in dealing with a heavier branch than usual. I was fascinated by the skill he displayed with his tools.

But on glancing down the line of trees he had already trimmed, a pang of remorse struck me. Stretching away into the distance was a pathetic row of trees all cut to a pattern and looking like some outsized parodies of the trees in a child's Noah's Ark set, all individuality cut from them, mere bleeding stumps which would struggle for a few years with a diminutive cap of foliage, then, should they fail to conform, to be ruthlessly removed. I suffered, as some of us do, when we see the interminable pacing of the caged polar bear, or the net-roofed aviary of an eagle in a zoological garden.

A healthy tree grown in well-tended woods also represents man's handiwork. It may be and often is a thing of beauty, but it seldom has the formation that nature had designed for it. By artificial means the evolution of the tree has now progressed along stereotyped lines, and if by chance it reverts to something suggestive of its original design, the forester proceeds to remedy this by mutilation to make it conform with his ideas of what it should look like or to make it of use to him. We therefore have to prefer ordered regimentation rather than haphazard quaintness.

How pleasant it is to be able to turn a corner and find some

tree that has grown quite free and as it pleases, even should
its form sometimes appear grotesque.

The time scale of trees is a longer one than our own. The
seasons have a more profound influence on them than on animal
life. The rising sap each spring is almost like a re-birth, the
only parallel in the animal world being the awakening from a
winter's hibernation. The condition is not analogous, because
the roots of the tree are partially active during the winter months
in all except arctic conditions. We have evidence of this in that
the trees can be severely pruned in winter on their exposed
portions and tolerate the treatment, but resent interference at
their roots, whether it be by man, burrowing animals or natural
causes. Rabbits can inflict serious damage by burrowing under
the roots of those trees which do not penetrate deeply into the
soil. The effect of these burrowings may be twofold, in that they
let in water which rests like a sort of cold poultice against the
roots, or the undermining may be such that in time the tree is
left standing on a sort of trellis work of roots like a daddy-long-
legs. This so weakens its hold on the ground that the first
severe gale uproots it.

Exposure to the elements is to some extent beneficial, in
that by its austerity it acclimatises the tree to meet the conditions
which perforce it has to accept. But, if too violent or too
severe, it inflicts damage either by dismemberment or stunting
the growth. There are numerous examples of the effects of wind
pressure along our coasts, where the trees can be seen so distorted
that they are useless for timber and pitiful to behold.

The obligation of immobility is the lot of all trees. Therefore
if the site of growth is unfavourable, the plant never has the
opportunity of developing as it should and is thus condemned to
deformity or early demise. Nevertheless immobility has certain
compensations if the site is well chosen : not only does the tree
benefit but many other living things do so as well. The tree may
become the home and shelter and security for nesting and roosting
birds, makes a suitable platform for bird song and provides shade
and warmth for many animals and other plants.

In old age many trees become host to parasitical plants—

ivy, mistletoe, lichens and finally to fungi. The last-named only appear in extreme old age and herald an early death. One of the first symptoms is a sudden growth of fungi round the area where the roots should be, followed by further invasion nearer to the trunk and finally to the bole of the tree itself. These fungoid growths are a depressing sight, but I do not think that they are of themselves injurious, they are merely an outward sign that decay has set in.

Ivy may be an adornment, but the tree which offers hospitality to it suffers grievous harm if the invasion is substantial, and in extreme cases strangulation occurs. It is kinder to the tree to remove ivy as soon as this plant appears, except in cases of extreme old age when the ivy may act like a bandage, give support to limbs that are hard and brittle and unable to survive without assistance ; but even under these circumstances the additional weight of the living bandage often proves too great a burden for the tree or its limbs to support.

Under the conditions by which we have developed our forestry we have so controlled the circumstances that the trees have to depend upon our assistance to prosper. This assistance requires some understanding if it is to prove effective. Trees are slow growers, so that experience in their culture is not acquired in a short time. Experienced foresters are men possessed of great patience and develop a philosophy to meet their calling.

Forestry is today a skilled profession, and the aims of instructors in the craft are to produce another raw material in a form that man can conveniently handle. The men employed in this profession are often sincere tree lovers, but they are so much under the influence of their craft that their ideas of a tree are limited and they see it as a commercial product : long straight boles, few branches and the crop all regimented together to facilitate the felling and disposal of the plants in their prime of life. To some extent I suffer from the same narrow outlook, dictated by the economic system of our times. The fact that we have to look on timber as a crop is bound to influence our outlook in a way that is regrettable.

I can still enjoy the task of collecting acorns and other seeds in the autumn, planting them and waiting for the result. With acorns the growth at first is remarkably quick, but the young oak tree slows down in the process of growth after the first exuberant rush at birth, and it takes a long time for it to attain sufficient stature to be planted out, and there to maintain itself in a wider world. Chestnut trees are quicker to respond both in the nursery and when planted out. To the youthful and aged enthusiast this is of some moment, as both exhibit impatience—the young because life seems so long, the old because it seems so short.

One of the major troubles with this fascinating ploy comes with the selection of the final site of planting. Space has to be allowed for future growth and the eyes of the child are often rather limited in their judgment of what space a grown tree will occupy, and so it often happens that at some future date mutilation has to take place to confine the tree to its immediate surroundings.

Tree cultivation by children is one of the very few joys that can be life-long. The ability of the tree to outlive its patron accounts for this; if the individual is fortunate enough to be able to see his handiwork in after years, the material aid to memory which the tree provides will bring a bright picture of the past to mind, and, to carry the idea to its logical conclusion, a tree makes a nicer monument than does a tombstone. For most of us the life of a tree is quite long enough to commemorate our existence and probably longer than our worldly accomplishments deserve.

CHAPTER ELEVEN

THE TICK

THE tick though of common occurrence in the Western Highlands does not seem to have inspired writers of natural history to give it the attention it deserves. Alas! neglect by the naturalist is not reciprocated by the tick, in his choice of a host for his parasitical habits.

Now I am interested in the tick, not because I think them beautiful, their habits pleasant or their mode of life admirable ; in fact, my interest is inimical to the tick.

In order to start this article I looked up the word ' tick ' in my dictionary, which tells me, ' The name common to certain small parasitical arachnidans or mites which infest sheep, goats, oxen, dogs, etc. . . .'

I was a little shocked to find that the eminent editor of my dictionary considered that I was one of the ' et ceteras,' because from time to time I have been ' infested ' (a nasty word) with ticks, perhaps it would be truer to say ' suffered occasional and isolated attack.'

Our home-bred ticks are of three varieties : there is the little black fellow, flat in construction and small in size ; then there is the grey kind of tick, obese when well fed—he is perhaps the commoner or more easily seen member of the family ; and finally there is the stag tick. This last insect may not be a tick at all for all I know, because he has very different habits from the other two, but he is always referred to as a tick by the unscientifically minded.

Fortunately all the ticks are only of seasonal activity, though in the case of the first two the season is a long one, April to November.

The little black tick has not quite the same repulsiveness in appearance as the others. Perhaps this is because he is small and his ugliness is thus the less apparent. If you subject him to close scrutiny under a magnifying glass, his hideousness is revealed.

He begins to wake up from his hibernal sleep about April; it depends to some extent on the temperature. He does not like cold nights, so that if there are April night frosts his season is delayed. He prefers to live in dry heather, grass or bracken when not accommodated on a host. I do not think he likes very damp ground, though it obviously takes a great deal of water to disconcert him, as the rainfall of his chosen country is on the high side. He is more active on his legs than the grey variety.

Now I too like to sit upon dry heather, grass or bracken when requiring rest on the hill, so we are bound to meet each other.

Most insect attacks make themselves apparent at the outset, such as the midge, the wasp, even the cleg though dainty in approach makes you aware of his presence at the start of the offensive. The tick does not. He crawls inside your clothing, and such is the delicacy of his tread and his feeding that even when he is piercing the cuticle you are unaware of him. It is not until you return home and examine yourself that you find him, head deeply sunk in your unresisting flesh. The ticks that attack humans are generally so small that removing them is a matter of some difficulty, because so little of them remains exposed once they have started their meal that there is nothing to catch hold of.

The grey variety of tick seems to prefer your dog to you. Whether this is because the lymphatic juices of the dog are more palatable to this kind of tick, I do not know, but it is a matter of some small satisfaction, because I find the appearance of the grey tick to be more revolting than the others. They are easier to remove from their host, because they leave an ample margin of protruding body outside the point of their attack, and the longer they have been feeding the grosser they become, until, towards the end of their repast they will almost fall out, which is I suppose what they do naturally if left undisturbed.

They are poor movers : their six little legs are able to propel them when they are thin and hungry, but once they start to swell their stomachs rest upon the ground and their legs wave feebly and quite ineffectively in the air, so that they must often have to rest content to stay in one place whilst digestion after a meal is in progress.

My dog rather resents their removal, especially if they happen to be newly arrived and still slim, thus more securely fastened to his person, but his dislike of the operation is probably due to the tick choosing the more tender places to attack. It often happens that when removing them the body of the tick parts from the head, leaving the head fast in the skin, which develops into a painful and inflamed lump. I believe it is better to allow the tick a short time in which to become satiated before the removal is attempted, however impatient you may be to extract them on discovery.

The stag tick is quite a different creature. To start with his season is short, August and September being the two months of his noticeable activities. Above all other differences he possesses wings. His attack is made from the air ; also he is very active on his legs, being able to move with some nimbleness ; he does not appear to be a blood sucker. I do not think he is so averse to damp or wet places as the other two, as I have found him more numerous in distinctly wet and marshy ground. He does not appear to bite his host, but he has very prehensile feet and he prefers to reside on your head. It is the hair he likes to hide himself in, but I can give no assurance that bald persons are immune from the attentions of the stag tick.

These ticks hunt in flocks and should you come across them the attack is in force, though they never aspire to the numbers of the midge hordes. It is the clinging propensity of the prehensile feet that I find so distasteful. You feel them alight and clap your hand to the spot, to discover a flat struggling crawly object that is difficult to remove.

The reason for the name ' stag tick ' is because they are particularly attracted by the fur of the red deer. In the stalking season deer are found to be infested with them.

I fail to understand why the stag tick requires a host, because as far as I know he does not feed off them, but perhaps I do not allow him sufficient time to start a meal.

Another puzzle to me is what the ticks do when no host is

available, and they must be comparatively rare events in the life of the tick, considering the country they inhabit. Do they go through long periods of austerity or do they find some alternative sustenance ? Most of our insect pests seem to be afflicted in this way ; perhaps that is the reason for the savageness of their assault. But I can never find the answer to these queries, nor do I know of any successful counter-measures which could be taken to defeat the attack, or, what I consider more important, how to lead an attack on the tick when he is passive, at home and hibernating.

It is quite probable that all species of tick lead an interesting life, of which I am quite unaware and which, if I knew it, would make them an entertaining study, rather than objects of detestation, but their virtues seem to be so hidden and their habits so repulsive, that however unbiased I would like to be I cannot look upon any of the ticks as other than vermin.

CHAPTER TWELVE

AN HOUR BESIDE A RIVER

THE scene of this rather idle hour was on the banks of a river in Iceland. The spot is a very pleasant one. From it no mark of man is visible; indeed the banks of this river throughout its entire length are but lightly touched by the hands of men and it is possible to find many such secluded corners. The landscape is just as it was before man came, and it now seems likely to remain like this for all time.

For six weeks absolute drought conditions had prevailed, and although there were many salmon in the river, fishing for them was but a mockery. The sun shone in a cloudless sky, no breath of wind ruffled the water. At the spot chosen, where there should have been rough and broken water with its accompanying song, there was only a gentle trickle which passed so quietly as to make no sound audible to my ears.

The waters of Iceland are particularly clear, soiled by no matter in solution or suspension, so that the pool, in spite of its depth of forty feet, was crystal clear and all its secrets were revealed. I could watch the salmon, the parr, an odd trout and a few migratory char resting in it. They were all quite undisturbed by my presence, and even if I was visible, which I doubt, I was accepted as part of the landscape and presumably harmless.

I fed one of the salmon parr, who accepted some crumbs from my sandwiches. He was both venturesome and greedy. The other parr were all too busy to notice my hospitality : they were taking some insects so diminutive that I was never able to discover what they were. The trout cruised around the pool looking for food, the char remained motionless and the salmon maintained themselves in a suspensory position about five feet below the surface, using their tails occasionally to counteract such current as there was and gently working their pectoral fins. From time to time they yawned, whether from boredom or, as I suspect, to increase the water flow through their gills, I do not know. One large cock fish was more persistent in this habit than the others, and even if he had not already been in plain sight the opening of that cavernous mouth would have revealed his presence, showing a white blot every minute against an otherwise dark green background.

Fascinating as they were to watch, after a time my attention wandered. All around me were numerous insects, whose exact species I was ignorant of, but on the ground spiders predominated, long-legged ones, rather slender in the body but remarkably active. They all seemed very busy. The reason for their activity escaped me, but quite clearly they were very much occupied. Some of them explored my person and my belongings, entering the fishing-bag and coming out only after the survey was complete.

Grey moths fluttered about rather aimlessly, their flight being somewhat like a primitive helicopter, always leaving me with the impression that flight is an adventure to them. They seem so insecure on their wings and at the mercy of the slightest puff of wind, which so often dashes them against the rocks leaving them maimed and broken, or carries them out on to the surface of the water, a medium in or on which they are in no way able to navigate.

The moth has a peculiar gamble with life, because he only survives maturity for so short a time, and it is pure chance whether his supreme hour is on a nice sunny warm day, in which he obviously revels, or one with a cold north wind off the ice floes. These latter conditions can give him no solace, but have to be endured for his few short hours. Unfortunately for him he has a different time scale from ours, and if his lot falls in weather such as I describe, he can never know the peace and comfort of a sunny day, so that he may welcome an untimely death as a release from a harsh and bitter world, however rude his passing may be.

A yellow bee seemed very busy. There was an intenseness about her occupation of collecting nectar, as if she knew too

well that the time for doing so was short, before she had to face
the bitter malignity of an arctic night ; to her,

> The winds of the world cried hurry
> The voice of the waters haste.

This insect world was even less conscious of my presence
than that of the fish.

I was visited by several species of birds. The ravens came
first ; they were hunting along the river banks, and as a matter
of fact they were old friends of mine. This family has, as its
hunting grounds, most of the river that I fish. I know where they
nest and I follow their activities annually, partly with an eye to
preserving any fish I may catch, because they like salmon and
unless I hide the fish they will devour it during my absence at the
next pool. Today although they saw me before I saw them, they
were confiding enough to come and sit on a hummock some fifty
yards away, and their croaking was but a mockery, croaking
ravens being supposed to ensure that the sportsman will have
success on the day on which the croak is heard. This is a legend
I was brought up on, but I now begin to doubt its accuracy.

The ravens were followed by golden plover, ring dotterel
and a pair of arctic skuas. The ring dotterel stayed for some
time. They were companionable and very confiding, coming as
close as twenty feet from where I sat, searching the stones at the
water's edge for food.

The river at this point runs between cliffs of imposing stature.
The rock being soft, the water has undercut them and formed low
caves, some of which are ten to twelve feet from back to front.
These caves at normal water-level are inaccessible. I had often
noticed that some species of bird was in the habit of using them.
This struck me as odd, because it seemed unlikely that they were
suitable for any form of bird life that I could envisage. Obviously
the birds using them were not small birds, the evidence on this
point being amply clear ; also this evidence clearly indicated a
water-feeding bird. Today the problem was solved for me : a
family of mergansers, mother and four young ones, swam up the
pool, solemnly climbed into the cave and sat in a row. Quite

why they did this was not clear, but from time to time one or more would go for a hunt in the pool, seeking small fish, return and waddle up the slope of the cave's floor and there rest a while. The low water-level enabled me to enter the cave, much to their consternation, but even when in it I failed to find its attraction. It was damp, sunless, dark and, to my nostrils, rather smelly, but this last detail might not have been obnoxious to mergansers. The only possible advantage that I could see that the caves possessed was that in normal water-levels it was a place of absolute security for them. They could enter and no enemy, human or otherwise, could ever approach them once they were within its dripping walls; furthermore it was not the sort of place that anyone would suspect of sheltering any animal life.

Of all the numerous living things that were visible at the river's side only the char, the salmon and myself seemed to be entirely idle. The first two were of course waiting, with a patience of unhuman endurance, until such time as they were ready for their reproductive effort—a wait that would extend for some further weeks. All the others were beset with industry of some sort.

Two hours passed in an idyll of contemplation and, although my purpose had been to catch a fish, a purpose which proved futile, seldom have two hours passed so pleasantly. I left the spot with reluctance, but with a sensation that all was well in a world where humans did not count for very much.

CHAPTER THIRTEEN

SALMON

THIS is not a treatise on the ecology of the salmon, nor is it instructive in the ways and means of catching these fish. About both these aspects in the story of the salmon, there already exists an ample literature.

Our knowledge of the life history of the salmon is largely incomplete due to his migratory habit. What happens to him in the sea still remains a mystery, occasionally enlightened by some brief point of light on a vast dark background, when a capture at sea is recorded. Such knowledge is rather like observational astronomy, where no telescope devised by man can enlarge a star to other than a point of light.

Quite apart from the ocean period there are phases during the mature salmon's river life about which our knowledge is fragmentary. To name three of these : 1. Why does the salmon leap ? 2. Why do they become ' stale ' ? 3. What are the facts about the period known as the ' mending of the kelt ' ?

I do not propose to answer these questions because I am unable to, but all three have intrigued me, and in the literature already published these three items are glossed over or ignored.

Why does the salmon jump in fresh water ? There are several theories on the subject, none of which seem to be very satisfactory. The suggestion that they do it to rid themselves of sea-lice does not seem to be the answer, because they go on jumping long after they are free from these parasites. To suggest that it is a habit that once acquired they cannot forgo seems unconvincing. Perhaps they like to keep themselves in training for surmounting some fall in the river, but this too seems improbable, because they jump after ascending all the falls and in waters which have no falls. The pleasure of a moment in the air may be attractive, but gravity ensures that the pleasure is but momentary and in no way similar to our own desire to dive into cool water when, however unpleasant the immersion, we are compelled to stay a few moments. A hooked salmon will jump at times, so it may be irritation of some sort, but again not every salmon hooked will jump, and, however lightly hooked, being attached to an angler must be a source of irritation long before it becomes one of fear. So why do not all hooked salmon jump ?

Jumping is not a newly acquired habit. The Romans gave the salmon the title of ' the leaper ' (Salmo-Salar), so it clearly is an inherited custom of long standing.

So far I have failed to find an answer that begins to satisfy me, but I have a faint feeling that he may leap from boredom, to enliven his long wait for the spawning season to arrive, or just to exercise those muscles which, during this wait, are idle and call for some demonstration of activity, purposeless as this action may be. But whatever the reason, the leap can be an impressive physical feat. I have seen a salmon clear fourteen feet in height from water surface to landing point, although this jump was to surmount a particular obstacle and not for mere pleasure.

Salmon anglers are happiest when they know that the water they are going to fish has just had a fresh run of salmon into it. They prefer that the fish should be just from the sea. In long rivers the upper beats seldom have this happy circumstance. The rods on these beats have to be content with fish moving up from a lower beat, and fishermen hope that the change of scene will have made the fish forget what flies and baits have already been offered to them and, should any fish have been hooked previously or pricked, that their memory is shortened or obliterated by the journey and the change of environment.

What it all amounts to is that we think, with some justification, that fish which have been in fresh water for some time are bad takers, a theory to which I myself subscribe. In August many pools are filled with fish that have been in the river for some months : we call them ' stale.' I wonder if this is a good term.

The reason for asking this question is that in my river in Iceland the same phenomenon is apparent, but in a very much

less exaggerated form than in the rivers at home, partly because the fish have not been in the water for anything like the same length of time as in the rivers at home and partly because the rivers are short, the water is cleaner and more turbulent conditions prevail.

The fish are not necessarily inactive when in this condition as they can be seen showing frequently, jumping, head-and-tailing and apparently stimulated by some urge, but at these times they are seldom interested in anglers' lures. All their actions deny the idea of ' staleness,' in fact, apart from running fish, they are often very much more active than they are earlier in the year when the water is colder and fresher; though the fresh feeling of cold water must be very different to a warm-blooded creature like man from what it is to one whose normal temperature is only about one degree Centigrade above that of the surrounding water and varies as does the water.

I am now inclined to think that this question of ' staleness ' is not that the fish are bored and have been overfished, but that it is a definite phase in the process of ripening to spawn.

This phase has to be passed through, and fish entering the river early in the season go through it in fresh water, autumn fish pass through it in the sea, hence late autumn fish are quite ready takers. Not that this fact is going to help us to catch salmon in low water in a hot August, but I find the idea interesting.

It would seem that to satisfy our curiosity the problem would have to be put to a zoologist. But if the theory is correct ' stale ' is not the word to use to describe the fish in this condition. If we must use this word in connection with living fish, it would be better used as an alternative to the word ' kelt ': not that we need another word to describe a spawned fish in fresh water.

The mending kelt has not had the thorough study that the fresh salmon has had. It is quite easy to understand why. The angler is not interested in him, so he is left to the gillies and the zoologists. The gillie too often has not the respect for this fish that is his due. The kelt is one of a thousand eggs that has reached maturity, overcoming countless hazards and has done his or her best to repopulate the river, therefore one to whom the most grateful thanks and gracious treatment should be accorded. We always hope that he may repeat the process, however unlikely the chances are that nature will permit him to do so.

The zoologist is more handicapped than the gillie, because so few of these fish come to his hands. Neither the nets nor the anglers are operating whilst the mending kelt is available and the only chance of contact is by observation of these fish in small rivers, which usually requires more time than the zoologist can afford.

I have been able to devote some time to the subject and find it is a most interesting study. But my knowledge is only the superficial one which observation of the fish in the water can give. The site of the redd is generally at some distance from what can be described as ' holding water ' for spent fish. The redd being in shallow water the spawning couple are sometimes nearly stranded, so after completion of the act they drop back to deeper and quieter conditions. This act of dropping, although a voluntary one, is dictated by the current. I only know of one place where the fish return upstream after spawning and this place is near the river's mouth, and there is no holding water between the site of the redd and the tide-way ; also the return to the pool is a very short distance, about a hundred yards.

On arrival in quiet water the fish pass through a period of complete dormancy. This may be from three to five weeks. The sexual attraction disappears, and I think that there is a progressive loss in condition. What factor decides the length of this period escapes me, but after it is over the fish becomes more active. This recovery of energy is particularly difficult to understand, because there seems to be no outside source of acquiring any in the form of food. It is also during this period that the kelt mortality is at its peak. Once this time is passed and the fish begins to take an interest in its surroundings, the long journey of dropping down the river begins. This journey is a slow one : the fish descends tail first, and it is not to be hurried by extraneous assistance ; in fact, any attempt to assist is resented.

The change in appearance begins at the same time, the hen

fish change first, losing the dirty grey colour on the stomach until a rather hard glittering silvery sheen is acquired. This change becomes progressively more noticeable day by day.

The last stage is a collection of numbers of fish in the lowest pools, where the final mending is accomplished. Considerable activity is often displayed : the fish may be seen jumping and are often mistaken for fresh fish by the uninstructed. Then quite suddenly they decide to leave for the sea. Twenty-four hours will clear these pools of kelts. A few of them may linger in the estuary, and I think that those who do this are fish that have not completely finished the process of mending, but cannot resist the temptation of following their companions. From then on they are lost to sight.

CHAPTER FOURTEEN

A SHORT COMMENTARY ON THE LIFE OF THE SEA TROUT

THE burn in winter has a chilly aspect, it is so apparently devoid of life, is inhospitable in appearance and its message is but a hint that you would be more comfortable in an armchair by your fireside than by its forbidding banks.

Yet within its heart there is life, for the most part dormant, but a close scrutiny and search can reveal some of the secrets. It is in these waters that the fertilised ova of the sea trout find refuge and security, tucked away between gravel-sized stones, awaiting the rise in temperature that will only come with the spring months before they can hope to hatch.

The ova when laid run certain risks during the winter period. These may be from purely natural causes, such as ice scouring, drought due to frost, and flood. The last is the most serious, because it is liable to wash the ova out from a position of security and deposit them on some land which under normal conditions is dry. There are risks from birds, rats and possibly eels, but for the most part these can be accepted without great fear that they will be catastrophic.

The moment the ova hatch and the alevin appears, one characteristic is abundantly clear : the little fish is dominated by the sensation of fear. This may be an instinctive reaction, but it is of primary importance for survival. One of the chief causes of this domination of fear is that the parents have long since departed, no parental protection is available. This is quite unlike most other living things on the higher planes of life. Very young birds, rabbits or other animals show no signs of it in extreme infancy. It is a little difficult to imagine a world in which fear is the first and most important sensation; it is certainly one which we can be thankful that our own progress in evolution has eliminated.

April, should the weather be benign, is when the alevins can best be seen. They select very shallow running water, preferably over gravel and where they can sun-bathe. For the first few days food is no problem because they live on the contents of the yolk-sac, which remains attached to them, and these contents are gradually absorbed by the growing fish.

At first the appearance of the fish is grotesque, the yolk-sac making their outline seem unbalanced, more like a disease than a sign of vigorous health. As the absorption takes place a gradually increasing urge of appetite makes itself felt, and the little fish begins to eat minute animalcula, at first automatically; but this automatic action soon develops into the normal hunt for food, stimulated by the independent thought and action of the individual fish. During the waking hours the whole life of the fish is dominated by the search for and the chase of food.

The change from the alevin to the fry stage is rapid, a matter of about ten days.

Once the fish has become a fry, a wider horizon becomes essential. The daily journeys become more ambitious, more water is explored and even some risks are run by sorties into deeper water, where there is an increase of danger. In this stage the little fish displays a growing confidence which is not always justified.

The burn on a warm sunny day in April or early May leaves on our minds a memory of pleasant tranquillity, but this cannot be the sensation left on the mind of the fish, because with growth and the ever-present urge for food, chances have to be taken in a world full of menace. Not only is there the risk of aerial attack but also underwater attack from larger fish and a number of other enemies. Fear, that was perhaps entirely instinctive at birth, must now have invaded such realms of consciousness as the fish possesses. What appears to be an idyllic condition to us observing from the bank, secure from the possibility of tragedy, is to the fish a period of acute mental alertness in order to survive, a state which humans rarely encounter except in wartime.

I am not quite sure that I can define the moment when a sea-trout fry becomes a sea-trout parr, but there must be a definite time and form of the change. Most observers rather slur over this point, as I have done.

When the parr stage is attained the burn is extensively explored, and during the summer months considerable distances are travelled away from the site of the redd where birth took place. Unless the redd was near the mouth of the burn, where it joins the river, it is doubtful if the parr will leave this water in its first year.

Summer passes in seeking food and yet more food, but as autumn arrives and the food becomes scarcer, a lessening of the activity of the fish is noticeable, and once the cold nights reduce the water temperature and with it the food supply a form of hibernation takes place. The parr seeks some stone and, by pushing, inserts his body into the cavity under the stone, and there prepares to pass the winter. He does not necessarily sleep, because, if he is disturbed, he is quite wide enough awake to swim away at great speed and find another retreat. Nevertheless the suspense in animation is profound, because I have found stones with fish under them which are not disturbed when the stones are moved slightly.

These resting places are to our eyes the acme of discomfort, the body of the fish is often so squeezed as to assume the appearance of well-packed sardines in a tin, and even the minor irregularities of the stone may be imprinted on the body of the fish. Perhaps the stone can be looked on as a blanket with the additional advantage of possessing the properties of armour as well.

Just as April is the month of hatching it is also about the time that the hibernating parr reappears, to spend another season in growing and probably descending to the river, only to hibernate —for want of a better word—for another winter.

That the one-year-old parr has a very complete knowledge of his local surroundings seems to be amply borne out by his actions, but to what extent he wanders is very difficult to determine. It now seems clear that in later life he will return to the same burn to spawn, so that if he possesses a memory this knowledge of locality, acquired in early youth, may be of value to him, but I find it difficult to assume that he has a memory; the return seems to be merely an inherited instinct of compelling intensity.

If the parr develops a wander-lust in his early fresh-water life it seems likely that he will leave the burn. If all of them were to stay there the food supply would be inadequate to maintain three and possibly four years' hatchings of ova.

Another remarkable contradiction in their lives is that though they are born in a crowd and for the first few weeks remain together, they develop individuality and independence in the search for food, only to give way once again to the herd instinct for the smolt migration. They retain this community life in the estuary, the sea and the return to the river. It is not until the act of spawning demands some privacy that they lose it, or until they have passed from middle to old age.

The very large sea trout are individualistic and seldom arrive from the sea in large groups, whatever they do whilst in the ocean. Perhaps having outgrown and outlived many of their own generation they have little patience with the rising one, and seek some solitude in consequence.

I find the smolt migration is of great interest. There are so many questions to which no satisfactory answer has yet been given. Some change in the development of the fish must produce the urge for this migration, but what this change is, or what stimulates it, escapes me. Why should it occur after two years of river life with some fish, three years in others and occasionally four years, before it is felt ?

The smolt gatherings begin late in April or early May, but the temperature of the water has some connection with the time selected. It is about the same time as the elvers enter the river. I think that these two migrations are only interconnected by the factor of temperature.

The parr begins to acquire the silvery coat which is essential to his protection in the sea some fifteen days before the great gatherings begin. It is noticeable that while the assembly is taking place the smolts are hungry, and for the period of the assembly some austerity has to be accepted, because the water selected for the rendezvous is not so abundant in food supplies as to be able to satisfy all these fish.

It is a little difficult to decide what actually occurs, because we have no means of knowing how long a particular group remains in the lowest reaches of the river. They may only be there for a day or two, and we see what appears to be the same group of fish for many days, whereas in reality the group we saw yesterday may not be the same as the one of today, the first group having gone on down to the sea, to be replaced by another company of young fish.

Once the tide-way is reached a profound change must be apparent to the fish. From having lived in the permanent draught of a one-way current, they now find still water conditions. The salinity of the water must upset their whole system, a fact we know from experiments carried out on smolts. The change to salt water must be gradual or the smolts die. Although food is now available in abundance it is of an unfamiliar appearance and no doubt taste as well. They at once become exposed to threats of which they have had no previous experience, nor do their former habits train them in any way to meet these menaces. There are no elder members of their race from whose experience, example or instruction they can learn anything. Is it then surprising that mortality among the smolts is high ?

The smolt remains in the estuary of the river for some weeks. This is curious, because it implies that smolts of different rivers acquire different habits. Many sea-trout rivers have no estuary, and fish of these rivers find themselves plunged into an ocean with surprising suddenness, a world of unbounded horizons, water of great depth, where pressure due to depth becomes a noticeable phenomenon. In the burn or the river the young sea trout has never had experience of any great depth of water. In rivers without an estuary the change in salinity is very abrupt.

The life now before the fish remains to us a mystery. We know that they grow rapidly and we know that they return to the river possibly as a finnoc in the late summer of the season of their descent, or they may stay a year at sea. What decides these returns is but a portion of the mystery. The reply often given,

that ' ripening to spawn ' is the controlling factor, is but half
the truth, and does not tell us what it is that ripens the fish ; also
many of the finnoc re-enter the river and have no intention or
ability to spawn the year of their first return. Why should this
be so ?

It seems improbable that the sea trout either takes the same
course or possesses the same habits as the salmon in the ocean.
They may well eat the same food whilst in the estuary and near
the coast, but the different time-table adopted by the two fish
suggests that they separate.

The sea trout is subject to the sensation of fear all his life,
but there is some amelioration in later life after he re-enters the
river. The portly trout is no longer subject to all the enemies
that his children have, though he never loses the instinctive
reaction of flight on the close approach of man or other large-size
land animals.

The elderly sea trout is a very valuable fish to the water he
inhabits. By his ability to reproduce many times in his life, he
is a potent factor in maintaining the stock, unlike the salmon
who is but rarely able to survive the exhaustive processes of
reproduction and recovery, or to reproduce a second time. It is
no uncommon occurrence to find a sea trout with seven or more
spawning marks on his scales, so as a kelt he should be treated
with the greatest respect; but this statement should not be
taken to encourage the mishandling of salmon kelts, who ought
to be given every opportunity to return if they can.

Should nature permit a natural death for the sea trout, this
usually takes place at sea, and we have no knowledge of how the
tragedy occurs, but what seems likely is that old age makes the
fish less active and possibly unresponsive to danger, so that he
falls a victim to a seal or other enemy, when his reflexes fail
either to deliver the message of danger or he is unable to respond
quickly enough after the message is appreciated. It is seldom
that we find many dead sea trout even in rivers thickly populated
by these fish.

CHAPTER FIFTEEN

THE EEL

THE Sargasso Sea occupies a large area of the western Atlantic Ocean, where ships seldom sail. It is an area of warm tranquillity in which large masses of Sargasso weed flourish. It also is the home of many varieties of marine life, and it is here that the eel spawns.

I have to confess that my knowledge of this area of the sea is slight. I have been there and seen it, but have no real knowledge of its inhabitants or their mode of life whilst living there.

To be authoritative on its inhabitants and their customs requires a long sojourn in these waters with a specially chartered ship. It is not a convenient hunting ground for ordinary mortals, so that the preliminary story of the life of the eel, as it is stated here, is for the most part based on the observations made by other naturalists better informed than I am, and for the rest it is what I imagine the eel does when in the Sargasso Sea and what his progeny do on their long journey from that sea to our waters.

The mass of ova of the eel must be of a specific gravity which permits it to remain near the surface of the water, probably among the weed to help in supporting it. The Sargasso Sea is deep, so that for the mass of ova to survive it cannot be of such a density as would allow it to sink, because if so, it would sink below the ocean current that carries the young to their destiny. Nor do I imagine that the ova or the young of the newly hatched eel are so constructed as to withstand the water pressure at great depths.

How long an ovum requires to hatch I do not know, but after hatching it seems that the young eel (not yet an elver) is quite helpless, though possibly capable of some movement, but in no way fit to compete with life in a hostile ocean. That he remains in or near the weed in his early post-ovum life seems probable, but because of the instinctive foresight of his parents he must be near to, or under the influence of, the current which for three years will be his home, and eventually bear him to our shores. That he feeds during this journey is obvious, as he grows and develops throughout the course of it.

Doctor Johannes Schmidt states that ' the initial movement of the young eel larvae after hatching is made at a depth of one hundred fathoms and in water of a temperature of 58° F. ; they remain at this depth under the influence of the current for several months ; after this period is passed they inhabit the upper strata of the sea, occasionally being found on the surface.'

The eel in the larva stage has long needle-like teeth. These are shed at the metamorphosis, which occurs in the change from larva to elver. The elver immediately grows another set of teeth in order to deal with the new foods necessary after the metamorphosis.

The three years' drift which begins at the nursery must be passed for the most part in a state of semi-consciousness, danger of attack never being appreciated and therefore never felt. The young eel does not at this stage of his life know the sensation of fear, which is quite unlike most other species of animal life on the same level of mental development.

The mortality during the passage must be tremendous and but serves to confirm the prolific nature of the mature fish.

The young eel must be very sensitive to changes of temperature, because this seems to be the only means he possesses to ensure that he remains in the current which bears him. Being incapable of much independent movement, he has to be aware of misdirection at an early stage, because once he became removed any distance out of the current it is doubtful if he would be able to regain it, so that minute changes of temperature must be felt and their warning acted upon. The appreciation of temperature is probably the only sensation of which he is aware during this stage of his development.

For nearly three years he passes a peaceful, fear-free, drifting existence, feeding automatically on plankton.

It seems to me that in the ocean passage he must progress at some depth below the surface, where the wind will not divert the little eels in their migratory journey and blow them out of the current. It is of course possible that many are thus destroyed.

As the journey progresses he must gradually become accustomed to the cooling of the water and very slowly become conscious of other sensations than temperature. At what age sight develops I do not know, but when he arrives at our coasts the elver can see, though not very well, and he has by then developed a sense of fear.

The elvers' arrival on our coasts and their entry of our rivers takes place about the end of April or beginning of May. What rules the dates is not understood, but it would appear likely that water temperature is once more the deciding factor for entering fresh water, and how they time the ocean passage to hit off this date is a mystery.

By the time he has reached the coast he has developed the ability of independent motion, and is able to surmount formidable adverse conditions but, possessing wisdom by instinct, chooses the easiest path to accomplish his purpose.

The choice of river seems to be to some extent haphazard, in that he probably ascends the nearest suitable river to his landfall. It is improbable that any other course is open to him.

Once the coast is approached the elver has developed to a stage in which he is conscious of danger. In the ocean the only menace, other than climatic, was from fish. As the land is approached aerial attack by birds constitutes another threat from another element and, for a short time, the peril is doubled. Once the river is entered the menace from fish is considerably reduced. Furthermore the river offers sanctuary, either in mud or stones where the elver can hide at no great depth ; also he travels in very shallow water where predatory fish cannot pursue him.

But he is then vulnerable to herons, water ouzels and other birds, though the toll taken by birds can only be a tiny fraction of the loss on the ocean passage. It would be interesting to know what the casualties are during the three-year migration, no estimate being possible, but they must be formidable. Even so, the numbers of elvers that run up our rivers can be guessed only in millions. On the river I know best, and it is a

small river, the elver run while it lasts is so great that no numerical estimate is possible.

The elver, once in the security of his fresh-water home, remains there for several years ; some observers suggest 5-8 years for males, 10-15 years for hens. The *Encyclopædia Britannica* states that there is an authentic case of an eel remaining in a pond for 31 years, an observation made by Dr Gunther, and such an authority on the ecology of fishes was not likely to have been mistaken.

He feeds and grows while in fresh water, though in northern waters the growth rate is not rapid.

His ability to cross dry land is so well known that it need not be dwelt upon here, except to say that the eel does not attempt a dry-land journey in absolute drought conditions. He must have moisture; a surface of dry dust will defeat him.

The return journey to the Sargasso Sea must be a great adventure. And on the rivers that have eel fisheries the adventure starts at once. The final migratory movement starts in the first October flood. The eel by this date in his migratory year has acquired the silvery coat which all sea-going fishes require to have. Hence the commercial name of ' silver eel.'

The journey by sea remains a mystery. After leaving the coastal shelf, at what depth does he travel ? Is it a communal journey ? And what is the final phase in his life? All unknown.

I think it is only during his last year or two in the river that he becomes the enemy of trout and salmon. I have never seen small eels taking ova from the redds, but once having acquired this taste he is voracious. I have seen eels eating ova behind spawning fish hour by hour.

The best method that I have found of defeating this robbery is to shoot them with a ·22 rifle. They are easy to shoot in shallow water, and it can be done without disturbing the spawning fish, as the eel stays some distance down stream of the spawners.

That the eel is a menace to fish culture cannot be denied, but his presence is not wholly bad. He destroys a number of other enemies of trout and salmon, and he provides a large portion

of the food for birds, which, if deprived of the eel, would attack
the fish we wish to preserve or their ova.

The eel has some peculiar habits. He is inclined to be
cannibalistic in captivity. In the Zoological Gardens in Edinburgh
I once saw one eel swallowing another almost of the same size
as himself. If I had not drawn the attention of the young lady
then in charge of the aquarium to the incident, I think both eels
would have died, but she was resourceful and equal to the occasion.
Using her knitting needles as a flagellant on the side of the tank,
she persuaded the eel to disgorge its companion and harmony
was restored. I am inclined to think that this cannibalistic tendency
is only shown in captivity where the individual becomes so bored
as to be reduced to this practice for entertainment.

The eel is a most interesting creature, and I have found some
considerable entertainment in the study of the elver by the
river side.

The first impression of them is one of feebleness and ineptitude,
but this is quite wrong. The elver at that stage is capable of
astounding acrobatics : he will surmount vertical obstacles even
though they be only damp. I have been at some trouble to place
obstacles in his way to see how he will surmount them, and so
far I have never succeeded in defeating him. Short of damming ·
the river and placing dry ashes in his path it does not seem possible
to stay his course.

I have tried to find out at what point in his river ascent he
decides to stop, but with no definite success, but I have found
eels of all stages of growth within 300 yards of tidal water,
so that it appears likely that he will stop just as soon as he finds
congenial living conditions.

The last phase in the life of the eel must be the most exciting
period of his life—the return to the Sargasso Sea, made this time
in the prime of his life, through several thousand miles of, for
him, uncharted ocean, against the current that bore him in
infancy, though it is probable that the mature eel does not travel
in the stream of the current on his return. How long a time
does he take to make the passage ? What adventures does he
encounter by the way ? Fascinating but unanswered questions.

For those who would angle for the eel, a worm is the best bait, though it is on record that an eel has been taken on a fly. In waters that hold eels there is no difficulty in making contact with him by means of a worm. It is the subsequent process of disentanglement that presents the problem. He has the ability to tie himself and the tackle into the most incredible knots. At the same time, he exudes a pernicious form of slime, which plays havoc with your tackle, contaminates your person and is excessively difficult to remove. In most cases the eel will be found to have swallowed the hook and some six inches of the cast as well, so that only a surgical operation will remove the hook and this operation can only be performed on the demise of the eel. To accomplish this, beheading seems to be the only successful method, in the process of which you sever the hook from the cast. The eel's tenacity of life is such that even after decapitation life remains in the headless body for some time, and the secretion of the slime already mentioned continues.

Much as I like eels to eat and to study, I now forego the pleasure of angling for them. It is the only pursuit I know where success becomes but bitterness and where failure is all joy.

CHAPTER SIXTEEN

BLIZZARD

FOR some days the thermometer had been registering a steady 72° F. of frost, or more colloquially described as ' 40 below '; the going had been good, the dogs fit and the only cause for anxiety for the two men on the trail was their own food supply, which, although adequate so far, was only sufficient if no accident befell them. They had hoped to replenish with meat before crossing the Divide, a hope that had not materialised.

The day's journey was over, the tent pitched and the Yukon stove was glowing red. On its top a kettle filled with snow was set to melt to provide water for coffee, the dogs were all picketed and fed ; in fact the day's work was done. There was no hint that any change in the normal routine was likely to occur. The only source of minor irritation was that the last loaf of bread had not been cut in slices before the start that morning, so that it was now frozen too hard to cut ; not even an axe would have made any impression on it. It was placed near the stove in the hope that it would thaw sufficiently to be sliced in the morning.

A last look out of the tent revealed a clear sky and many stars, a few wisps of aurora and absolute stillness of air, the dogs all asleep, and nothing seemed to disturb a darkened world, frozen into immobility. In fact the prospects for the continuation of the journey looked to be set fair.

At five o'clock in the morning the stove was rekindled, the temperature in the tent having dropped to about zero, but wrapped in their wolf robes neither man had felt any discomfort. With the stove's heat the conditions improved. Outside the tent it was still as dark as ever ; indeed there would be no increase in light for many hours, and even then the daylight would be subdued. The sun would not rise above the horizon for the place was too far north.

The preparations for the journey were made. No longer were these anything but a matter of routine, long familiarity having destroyed any romance that once might have been felt in these actions.

At 6.30 a.m. the tent was struck, the sled loaded and the dogs harnessed. The hollow where the tent had been was now but a soiled blot on a clean landscape, and the hospitality it had offered was of the past. The next fall of snow would obliterate all traces of a small corner that, for a few hours, had provided rest and shelter for two wearied men and their team.

The landscape was bleak, unrelieved by hills or any other dominating feature ; such undulation in the ground-level as existed was no obstacle to progress. There were many small frozen lakes and a few scraggy birch trees and jack pine, all that could be expected on the edge of that imaginary line—the ' northern limit of trees.' Such examples of these plants that were to be seen, were stunted parodies of what a tree could be, never in that climate to become anything else. The ground was snow covered but not deep snow, making the trail easy and not deep enough to necessitate the wearing of snow-shoes, or to have to break the trail for the dogs. The snow-shoes were lashed on the top of the sled load, handy in case they might be required later in the day.

The only sounds were that of moccasined feet on powdery snow, the slight hiss of birch wood sled runners and the occasional word of command to the lead dog.

The trail led them by a rather tortuous course to avoid nigger-heads and to make use of the frozen lake surfaces as much as possible, so that the actual course chosen was longer in distance than a direct path. Time would be made up by the speed that the easier surface allowed.

They were making for the river, because a frozen river course is the easiest road for winter travel and nearly all human settlement is by its banks. The distance they still had to travel was calculated in time rather than mileage, the unit being days rather than hours.

At 9 a.m. a halt was called to rest the dogs, examine their

feet and check the harness, all routine duties.   The sky had by
now lost its aspect of complete darkness, though it could not be
said that it was light.   There was, however, a lessening in the
profundity of the darkness and—one barely noticeable change—
it seemed to be getting warmer.   At first nothing ominous could
be attributed to this sensation ;   in fact it was rather welcome.

After another two hours of travel the light had developed into
the typical arctic winter's day, making the scene even more
inhospitable than before light was shed upon it.   The absence of
contrasts in the surrounding country was very marked, yet, like
startling silhouettes, the dogs, sled and the two men stood out
on this white background, only relieved by slight changes in tone
where the stunted trees, rimed with hoar frost inches long, made
a slightly greyer tone on the blue-white snow.

A glance at the thermometer revealed a rise in the temperature
of $7°$ F. and a few minutes later a thin fall of snow began.   This
in itself was not serious, but should the snow continue it would
make the going harder.

The two men looked at each other but said no word.   Both
were experienced arctic travellers;   both knew the risks entailed.

The snowfall increased; heavier flakes were now falling—rather
gobby flakes.   This heavy type of snow very quickly makes the
going bad; an hour of it would necessitate snow-shoes and trail
breaking.

Just as they came to the decision that snow-shoes were
necessary, a faint breeze sprang up.   In arctic countries it is
noticeable that when the thermometer is very low there is no
wind, a most fortunate provision of nature, because wind is the
element that makes the cold really felt.   Ten degrees below with
a wind feels infinitely colder than $40°$ below in still air.

Once again these men exchanged glances, and perhaps in them
were the first signs of a realisation of what might lie ahead.   A
wind with this type of weather implied no easy passage and might
contain the threat of real and deadly peril.

Here there was no shelter.   It seemed wiser to ' mush ' on
and to seek a corner where a camp could be located, there to
stop and shelter until the weather improved.   But such a halt

could not be for very long, because the food supply prohibited any protracted delay.

The cold now seemed intense, though the thermometer was only reading 25° below, a rise that presaged no good. The snow flakes ceased to be gobby and became finer in texture, no longer just floating down but slanting, driven by a wind.

This wind, though as yet not strong by any reading on the Beaufort scale, was clearly increasing. Little puffs of fine powdery snow were being swept along the surface of the ground. Slight as these were, it was already painful to look into the wind, a sure sign that the time was at hand to stop.

It is these fine driven ice particles that constitute the menace of a blizzard, and it is because of them that the traveller loses his way. The reason for this is not far to seek: as the wind increases so do the quantity and velocity of the particles, so that the traveller can no longer look up. He keeps his head down, and there is no surer fact than that a man or a beast with his head down cannot keep a straight course. He walks in a circle. The curve may be of large diameter at first, but as fatigue, cold and ever decreasing range of vision develops, the smaller in diameter becomes the curve.

There is only one answer. While still fit to do it, shelter must be contrived and the journey suspended. The inexperienced fail to realise the moment when such action is vital, the result—tragedy.

In selecting a site to make a camp some care has to be exercised : shelter other than the thin canvas of the tent's walls is very essential if the tent is to resist the wind and the piling effect of blown and falling snow. Especially is this so if it has to weather the ferocity of an arctic storm. Our two travellers knew the risks and the essentials, but this knowledge is not in itself sufficient. Some outside help from the contours of the country is essential.

The remark ' We must camp ' was almost trite, and the reply, ' Yes, but where? ' was but the measure of both their thoughts.

The dogs were as sensitive to the menace as were the men, and there was a tendency among them to stop, a tendency harshly but necessarily checked.

After another hour of rather laborious travel, where very little progress in distance was made, they came upon a slight bank which gave some break to the direction of the wind. Here they stopped.

The unloading of the sled, picketing of the dogs and pitching of the tent was a slow and painful business. The wind, now strong, made the handling of any articles an agony. The hands had to be taken from the big trail mitts, and before all the work was done both men had frost-bitten fingers, the thawing of which is painful, though under these circumstances such an accident is quite usual and not of itself very serious.

The wind increased and in an hour's time it was impossible to see where the dogs were lying or to see the tent from a distance of a very few yards.

During the following three days the wind blew unceasingly and with considerable violence. The cold increased. To go outside the shelter of the tent was to expose the whole body to its blast, and chilled the individual to his very marrow. Yet they had to go out from time to time, to feed the dogs, to see that they were not buried and to attend to the security of the tent. All these duties involved some risk other than the cold : even in the short distances of travel required it was quite easy to miss the way back to the tent, and once a sense of direction is lost, so too is the individual.

The whirling mass of frozen particles and snow reduces visibility to zero, an effect quite apart from the painful and blinding impact of these particles on the eyes.

Fuel and food both began to run dangerously low, and the two men were not half-way upon their journey at the rate of travel that would now be forced upon them.

These two men were not novices in the ways of an arctic winter, but anxiety began to dominate all other considerations. Like most arctic dwellers they were silent most of the time, finding companionship without conversation sufficiently satisfying, but as the hours went by the anxiety of each became so persistent that some talk was a relief. The talk, such as it was, was mono-syllabic and referred to the essential details necessary for survival—

food, fuel, the condition of the dogs and where the nearest point of succour could be found.

The arctic trails are lonely, human habitations are rare oases, and those who travel these trails have to depend for the most part on their own resources.

After three days there seemed to be a slight reduction in the wind, and, as the food situation had deteriorated from inadequacy to scarcity, a decision had to be made. Were they to try and march again? Or were they to remain where they were? Both courses had something in their favour but both held the gravest perils.

It is seldom possible to forecast the duration of a blizzard, and whereas it is folly to travel at the height of such a storm, any lessening of its ferocity tempts the traveller, who is short of food, to try and continue so as to reach some place of security.

It was now clear that unless the blizzard died out, they would be without food. No-one can travel far on an arctic trail in winter and expect to survive for long, unless he is well nourished.

These men were not such as would fear to make a decision, and once come to they would carry it out with determination, so they decided to make the start. One of the dogs was found to have a bleeding lung, due to the cold. It was unfit for harness and was shot. This, though unfortunate, because the pace would be reduced and the strain on the remaining dogs increased, also meant that the dogs that were left would have a slightly increased ration.

The struggle to reload was worse than they expected, even though the partial lull in the wind was noticeable. Slowly the sled was got under way. Once started the conditions improved slightly, probably due to the stimulation of movement, but trail breaking was a wearisome labour and the wind bit sorely, making their eyes ' rheum ' and the salt tears freeze on the cheeks below. All the forenoon the struggle went on, then one of the trace-dog's feet began to freeze. This condition of frost is complicated with snow-balling between the pads, forming solid ice lumps which cut the pad. In fair-weather conditions it can be remedied by putting moccasins on the dog, but once the weather is really bad, the dog is not only useless, but a further burden to the rest of the team.

This dog also was destroyed.

Camp had to be made early, as by now the team were reduced to five dogs. It was clear that if the journey was to be continued, some of the gear would have to be jettisoned—a hard decision to make, as only essentials had been included in the original loading.

That night the wind increased again, and in the morning it was all too clear that no start could be made. The daily ration was cut down to but a third of what could be considered adequate. Another night followed by a start late the next morning.

The feet of one man froze that day, and he had to ride for long periods on the sled step and was quite unable to take his turn at breaking trail. The lead dog died in the traces—a very serious disaster. Only a few miles were covered.

Both men developed bad face cracks, and the frozen feet were clearly a case for surgical treatment. Still they struggled on. The fifth night saw them too weak to pitch the tent and the fuel supply was now very short. Not that there was no fuel about, as the few trees could provide this, but only so long as the men were fit to cut and collect it. This was no longer the case.

On the sixth day they were unfit to travel. It seemed all too likely that all that might ever be found of them, was a hand stuck out of a snow drift, or, in the summer two skeletons lying beside a deserted sled, if indeed they were ever found.

Late on the sixth day the blizzard ended, the wind died down and silence reigned supreme once more over that white and bitter land. They were too weak to make any move. . . .

By pure chance an Indian, at the extreme limit of his trap line, found them and thus salvation came.

> The blizzard passed and dawn broke, knife-edged and crystal clear ;
> The sky was a blue domed ice-berg, sunshine outlawed away ;
> Ever by snowslide and ice-rip, haunted and hovered the fear
> Ever the Wild malignant poised and panted to slay.

An arctic blizzard is no fun: it entails a bitter fight for survival against a malignant, impersonal, relentless and, too often, a conquering foe.

CHAPTER ˙SEVENTEEN

The Taxidermist

I ONCE read a story for children about a magic toy shop, where the most delightful and incredible adventures happened. I know just such a shop, though it does not deal in the same kind of toys nor do quite the same adventures occur within its doors.

I had better admit at once that I have never outgrown the mentality of the child, or else I have passed to that second stage in the condition without observing any intervening period.

There is a quiet street in Edinburgh whose noble buildings emphasise the solid respectability of the quarter. For the most part these edifices are occupied by large firms whose financial stability appears to be beyond dispute. Others have brass plates indicating that members of the more distinguished professions are to be interviewed in them. In yet a few more of these buildings there are shops on the ground floors, shops of the very best and most exclusive character. In these emporiums there is no crowding, no queues line the pavements of this street. Should you be bold enough to enter one of these shops, impecccable service marks the way you are greeted. It is not the kind of shop in which you produce a purse or hurriedly search your pockets for small change. If you have been so rash as to make a purchase you will have to fill in a cheque, and the problem that then confronts you is how many digits to add to the first figure you have written. It is a very nice street.

Half-way along its southern side there is a forgotten building— a relic of a past age; quite why it is still standing is a little difficult to find out. It is rather shabby—like an elderly lady who has a very small annuity living among her very prosperous grand-nephews.

This house has a basement and in this basement lives the taxidermist. It is true he has a window facing the street, but

it is so far below the ground-level that it assumes the appearance
of a sky-light rather than a window. It is incredibly dirty.
Cobwebs of unknown vintage festoon its lintels. Just inside the
window and faintly visible is a stuffed starling; at least it used to
be a stuffed starling, but in the passage of years since I first saw
it the dust has so accumulated it now would be hard to say what
its species was. But I think it is the same starling because, judging
by the dust, it has not been moved for a century or more, and in
the dim past its species was identifiable.

Should you have occasion to enter the shop, the door protests
at your passage, and inside there are strange things: birds of
quite incredible plumage, beasts with queer heads, fishes of all
shapes, serpents, insects and dried vegetable matter; at the far
end of the room a bench with old-fashioned tools. The general
impression is one of complete chaos. There is a very small
portion of a counter kept clear of debris where the owner of the
establishment is accustomed to look out upon his visitors and to
take the small sums of money he charges for his handiwork.

The place is supervised by an incredibly old man; I have
known him for fifty years. My earliest recollection of him was
that he was a survival from one of the early Biblical characters,
rather like the picture of Moses in my child's Bible. He looks
exactly the same today. He wears a skull cap, steel-rimmed
spectacles with thick lenses, a black alpaca coat and a once-white
carpenter's apron.

He is quite charming. His knowledge of natural history is
profound. How he acquired this escapes me, because he never
seems to have ever left his shop. Perhaps he is a great reader,
but from his conversation it would appear that he is no stranger
to the countryside, nor is his knowledge confined to the British
Isles. Should you speak of polar bears in northern Alaska he
seems to be on intimate terms with them, and he can discourse
about the swamps surrounding Lake Gatum. Such is his address
you would think he had been in both places last week.

He is a superlative craftsman. All his work exhibits the
touch of a master hand, his creation of surrounding detail so
fitting to the subject that it leaves you with the further conviction

that only a man who has actually seen and experienced the conditions could execute it.

A visit to the shop is one of pure delight. There is no sensation of hurry about the affair; a discussion of any natural history subject is welcome to him.

In this queer backwater a visit to tropical jungles, arctic barrens and strange wild rivers is possible all in the space of an hour, and on leaving it seems like waking from a dream or the return from a visit to a weird kind of fairyland.

Although the shop looks like a forgotten corner in Bedlam, there is some sort of order, because the old man never loses specimens sent to him, and the finished work is packed and wrapped in new wrappings. He may be out of keeping with his neighbours, but he is eminently respectable, trustworthy and, for all I know, as financially sound as the greatest of them.

If I am condemned to spend any length of time in that city, a visit to his shop takes me on magic wings to other lands, and in spite of its smell of decaying bodies, dust and the preservatives of an alchemist, the sounds of rivers, grinding ice floes, or of duck flighting, can at will be heard.

Each year I expect to see the establishment closed and I approach the sunken basement in fear lest the old man has at last failed to weather another winter. With his passing I feel sure the place will disappear. Never has an apprentice worked there. No child or grandchild is ever to be seen. Even if the place is a magic shop, I suppose the owner is mortal.

CHAPTER EIGHTEEN

THE SCALE OF TIME

WE are so accustomed to thinking of time in our own terms that we forget or completely disregard the fact that other forms of life probably have a very different appreciation of this dimension. In point of fact we use two scales to measure time: the first, an arbitrary one, based on solar and terrestrial phenomena of which the units are from seconds to years; the second, a pleasantly vague one, which is based upon our own feelings. Its units are infancy, childhood, youth, middle age and old age, with some consideration being given to the seasons, though we ignore the fixed dates laid down by learned astronomers as to when these seasons begin and end. To illustrate one anomaly in this arrangement, the official summer begins on 22 June and midsummer day is also said to be on this date.

I am not trying to advocate any change in the arrangement. To alter our own system or to reduce the number of its units would be as futile as to suggest that linear distances should be measured only in Angström units or mega-parsecs.[1] But we should have an open and understanding mind of the scale on which the subject of our interest is living.

Many insect specimens after their metamorphosis are unconscious of darkness. In this phase of their existence they are born to and die in such a blaze of light as our climate permits. Darkness, as we understand the term in everyday life, is an unknown condition to them. To travel farther afield, at great ocean depths many species that dwell in them are unaware of light. No rays of which we are conscious can penetrate to the abysmal depths in which they live. Furthermore they have no seasonal

---

[1] The Angström unit is used for the measurement of light waves ; it is $1/254,000,000$ of an inch. The mega-parsec is the astronomical unit for measuring very great distances ; a parsec is 3.3 light years or 19×10^{12} miles, a mega-parsec is 1,000,000 parsecs.

or other changes of temperature: their lives are passed in a constant state where the thermometer perpetually reads between 3° and 4° F. above the freezing point of water. If we lived under these conditions it is certain that two of our yard-sticks for the measurement of time would be missing.

Coming higher up the scale, we are all familiar with the statement that one year's life in man is equivalent to seven years of the life of a dog.

Let us pause a moment to consider seven years' experience crowded into twelve months. All pleasures would be fleeting indeed: a restful nap of twenty-one minutes is reduced to three minutes; no sooner are the eyes closed than we are awake again. The passage of active bounding life passes to infirmity and the stiffness of old age, almost in a flash.

This acceleration of the scale of time becomes the more marked as we travel down the table of longevity.

We live near the summit of this scale. There are a few mammalia and many plants that are above us on the list, for whom the velocity of time is more leisurely by most of the standards which they can appreciate, though the passage of the seasons and passing of the days will be on a quicker tempo to fit in with their life span.

It is rather as if some magic drug, as portrayed in H. G. Wells's story, 'The New Accelerator,' was available, and a draft or drafts of variable potency would transport the patient on to whatever rate on the scale he wished to investigate.

I think we cloud the issues in our minds by omitting to consider time as a variable dimension. To sit, god-like, wearing a cloak of false immortality, whilst studying a short-lived species may be very pleasant, but it is apt to make our conclusions misleading.

Is time a dimension of constant velocity? As this is no place to discuss an abstract problem in either metaphysics, philosophy or pure mathematics, it had better be left to those who are very much more competent to deal with it, but if what has been said will make the reader pause for a moment, the meditation thus enforced may benefit or amuse him.

CHAPTER NINETEEN

SOME NOTES ON OBSERVATION

ALL roads to knowledge are long and strenuous. Many of us find some of these paths dull, but the road of the natural history student is a pleasant one, and the obstacles with which it is strewn are but stimuli to further effort.

Nature has a habit of concealing secrets from the idle or the casual eye, and demands that effort by the student is part of the price he has to pay before the information is delivered.

There are two varieties of this study, the first being that of the scientist, who nearly always brings to the pursuit the value asked of him in patience, persistence and hard work, so it is not for this class of student that these notes are written. The second class are the great majority of us, who in daily country pursuits wish to learn more of what happens in that world which we see, but are not part of, though some of us pass along the fringe of it in the pursuit of our pleasure or daily work. Man has chosen or been forced to adopt a line of evolution which inevitably segregates him from the inhabitants of the natural world and to whom, on the whole, he is a hostile influence.

A better understanding of natural history at an earlier date might have saved much that is now irretrievably lost, and today it could save much that is shortly to be condemned.

The beginner starts with scales upon his eyes, and the time taken for these scales to fall depends upon the aptitude of the student and in whose footsteps he follows. So much of the available evidence is circumstantial, and the story has to be read partly by inference. Part of the legal definition of circumstantial evidence is so apt that no apology is made for quoting it : ' Facts cannot lie, but they may and often do deceive.' It is in the interpretation of the facts that experience and training count for so much.

In the casual or intermittent study of nature it is easy to slur over the evidence, and the slovenly observer walks past the clues without ever perceiving a story that lay open to him, if he had but taken a little more trouble to see and think about it.

It must not be imagined that each sortie of the observer, however keen, sharp-eyed and industrious he may be, will reveal some secret. It is probable that, as in a day's fishing, the basket will be empty, or only a small fraction of evidence will be offered, leaving a crumb to be gathered, stored in the mind, or, if this be a doubtful recording apparatus, a note book, and when further pieces of the mosaic are available, the whole may be built up into a consecutive and balanced truth.

Direct evidence is seldom available, yet a story is told, writ in sand, mud or grass, where events have happened. We must read these signs and build up the story from these circumstantial clues.

So many of the facts exposed are the signs of tragedy, perhaps because they are the easier to read : a dead body, a whitened bone, a tuft of fur or a bunch of feathers, all surrounded by signs of violence—almost the perfect setting for a novel of detection—but there are no witnesses who can speak. The story, if it is to be read, has to be deduced by the observer, and on his acumen and past knowledge will depend its veracity.

If blessed with acute senses the observer is endowed with a good starting-point, but it takes time to attain proficiency in the use of them ; the process will not be hurried.

The habit of moving by stealth must be acquired, but only in the initial stages need this movement be slow. After some skill is possessed not much time need be lost in the approach.

Some of the American Indian hunters have developed the rapid silent approach to a remarkable degree, but this is not a prerogative of theirs. The white man can do it too. Where the white man fails is in the ability to stay immobile for hour after hour, without the apparent movement of an eyelid, in extremes of weather and in the acme of discomfort. I think it is this one factor that makes them superior to most white hunters in the study of the species they know best.   The Indian is a hunter, rather than a naturalist.

The casual naturalist, as opposed to the scientific one, is following a wider but less detailed study, therefore his knowledge is picked out from nature in smaller scraps.   A walk along the river bank has so many facets—the ecology of the fish, birds, insects and animals, each detail being considered—where the scientific observer disregards all except those of his study of the moment, the selective search as opposed to the general search.

A day's fishing may so absorb the mind of the angler that for most of the day he is concentrating on flies, baits and their presentation, or his skill in the art of casting.   There is no room in his mind to give to what he considers extraneous detail, but if, from time to time, he will pause and let a few symbolic scales drop from his eyes, he will be none the worse, rest his water and improve his basket.

The hunter, whether of fur, feather or fin, becomes the better naturalist if he will retrace his steps over the ground of his hunting in the off-season, without gun, rod or other implement of the chase.   Where his mind is not set upon destruction and is thus free for observation, not only will he find a deeper vision but a greater understanding, and become the better hunter in consequence.   The scrap of detail acquired today may be of no significance, but tomorrow, it may be the missing piece of the puzzle, and as such is eagerly acclaimed to round off a picture of absorbing interest.

There is a considerable difference between the observer and the hunter.   The hunter is out of set purpose : he is endeavouring to add to his supply of food, secure a trophy or fulfil an acquisitive purpose other than the search for pure knowledge.   To succeed in this, many of the qualifications of the naturalist are of use to him, but his whole being has to be concentrated on the chase.

The true naturalist has to be something more than a man of action, he should be a finely-tuned recording instrument, a sort of aeolian harp ready to be played on.   The incomplete and abstruse message, which may be all he will receive at any given moment, demands precision in the recording machine, delicacy in appreciation and imaginative realism.

In this fact lies one of the pleasures that can be enjoyed. The element of surprise is there and, unlike the hunter's, can be appreciated for a longer time. Such a condition of mind is subject to no sudden termination by the discharge of a firearm, or put to flight by some error in the stealthy approach for the fell purpose of destruction. Should the observer have to make a nearer approach which fails, the subsequent anti-climax is less disastrous.

The fault of over-eagerness is one of the early pitfalls. Another is the too ready acceptance of a solution without due weight being given to the evidence. The evidence gives the facts, the observer tells the story and the tale should not be told too hastily.

Few tools are required, but the obvious items, field glasses or stalker's telescope, are worthy of the burden they entail. Not so obvious is a small magnifying glass ; it is of no weight to carry. If the study of rivers interests the would-be naturalist, a pair of polarising glasses will be found invaluable. Beyond these items no additional equipment is necessary. Proficiency then depends entirely on the aptitude and enthusiasm of the individual.

Books on natural history help to stimulate the beginner and are of great assistance to the expert, even when only used as books of reference, though most of them can be delightful reading in themselves, and their reading will help to uncover lost and forgotten details in the store-room of the mind.

CHAPTER TWENTY

PROGRESS

A FUNDAMENTAL difference between ourselves and the animal world lies in the interpretation of the word ' progress.' This word to all except man has no meaning. The only human analogy that I know of is to be found among the Esquimaux who have no word for ' war,' because they have never known such a catastrophe, and hence have coined no word to express an action completely outwith their experience.

Humans lay great stress upon this quality of ' progress.' They are always striving to acquire its imagined benefits, or forward the aims that they embody in this word. I do not think that they are any happier in consequence ; indeed each so-called advance in progress seems to bring anguish in its train. There are, of course, a few benefits, and for these rare prizes our discomfort will continue, because once launched on this hazardous path of experiment we cannot stop.

All other forms of life disregard it completely. The birds sing the same songs that they did a thousand years ago. The salmon migration is the same as it was at the beginning of recorded time. The nests of the birds are subject to no planning committees, nor are they harassed with permits and other irritating and frustrative items.

Yet we live in communities just as some other animals; community life is no strange way of living to many species. The good of the community is considered and certain laws are immutably accepted so that the race may continue. Socialism appears to work well where it is not another word for jealousy, which is the driving power behind so many of our own socialists. Anarchy, a prevalent theme today, is unknown in nature, but we have developed a system where many people wish to destroy all

existing laws and institutions, and not till this destruction is complete do its advocates suggest rebuilding.

In fact we are so over-burdened with the necessity for progress we have largely lost the fun of living, as well as the true meaning of the word ' progress.'

In using the word progress we must not confuse it with evolution, a stern and immutable process upon which man has little influence, because evolution is slowly taking place all the time. Even if it is not appreciable in short periods of 1,000 years, it undoubtedly is noticeable in 1,000,000 years. But the process is so gradual that no individual member of any species can detect it. Change is often resented provided we are aware of it, but should change be so gradual that we do not notice it, we may welcome these gradual changes which provide no shock to our senses.

Life in the animal world is only subject to the gradual change which evolution entails, and I can only contemplate their mode of life with unbounded envy. Youth in man is the period when violent change of an existing system seems desirable. This is rather curious to think about because it is peculiar to man. Admittedly animal youth may exercise less restraint than their elders, be adventursome and possibly wish for an alteration in the existing régime, but such extravagances are never allowed to imperil the structure of the way of life of the species.

It is possible that if we were dependent on the outcome of evolution to bring progress, many of us might complain of monotony in life, but the urge to change destroys so many of the pleasures that surround us, the urge itself prohibiting our having time to see and enjoy them.

A study of nature need expend neither coupons nor cash, and there is much to see and more to learn for anyone who will take the trouble to study what is happening daily in the countryside, be it in a garden, a hedgerow or, for the more fortunate who live in or can visit, wider and less confined spaces.

No pleasure can be expected without some payment, but the only fee required for this study is a receptive mind, alert senses and patience.

The blackbird of today sings the same song as his forbears did before the Roman Conquest ; his song is still one of pure delight to us.   How many of our own works of art will, after that length of time, still be appreciated?   The clothing of our birds has not followed any transient fashion, and they are still beautiful ; so too with the flowers, the trees and many other species.   It is something to contemplate and marvel at.

It would appear that only man has any necessity for such a word as ' progress.'   It would do no harm if, for a space, this overworked process were allowed a rest.

www.ingramcontent.com/pod-product-compliance
Lightning Source LLC
Chambersburg PA
CBHW030148310326
41914CB00086B/38

* 9 7 8 1 4 4 6 5 0 4 2 9 1 *